Reasoning and Writing

Level F
Textbook

Siegfried Engelmann

Bonnie Grossen

SRA

A Division of The McGraw-Hill Companies

Columbus, Ohio

Cover Credits

(l) Artville, (r) PhotoDisc.

SRA/McGraw-Hill

A Division of The McGraw·Hill Companies

Send all inquiries to:
SRA/McGraw-Hill
8787 Orion Place
Columbus, OH 43240-4027

Printed in the United States of America.

ISBN 0-02-684795-7

1 2 3 4 5 6 7 8 9 VHJ 06 05 04 03 02 01 00

Lesson 1

Part A

- Words in sentences have different parts of speech.

- Some words are nouns. There are different ways to test for whether words are nouns.

- Here's one test: If the word you're testing make sense with the word **one** or the word **some** in front of it, it's a noun. Nouns name something that you can count or point to. So **one** or **some** makes sense in front of a noun.

    Examples:
    beautiful
    situation
    sand
    people

Part B

Test each word to see if it's a noun. If it is a noun, write the word **one** or **some** in front of it.

Sample Word   milk

1. quickly	7. always
2. beautiful	8. events
3. argument	9. noise
4. water	10. north
5. seeds	11. old
6. hungry	12. sister

For each item, if Fran says a complete sentence, don't write anything. If she says part of a sentence, write the complete sentence.

1. Don: Where did you go yesterday afternoon?
    Fran: To the fair.

2. Don: You said that you were going to go to the mall with me, but you didn't even call me.
    Fran: Sorry about that.

3. Fran: It slipped my mind.

4. Don: That makes me mad. You weren't very considerate.
    Fran: You are right.

5. Don: Who went to the fair with you?
    Fran: Mike.

6. Don: Well, why didn't you invite me to go along with you?
    Fran: I told you that I forgot.

7. Don: You really like Mike better than me, don't you?
    Fran: That is not true.

8. Don: Well, we could go someplace next Saturday. Where would you like to go?
    Fran: The mall.

Part D

- Statements are **more general** if they tell about a larger number of things.

- Here's a statement:

  They walked into Edna's house.

- Here's a **more general** statement:

  They walked into a building.

For each item, write **A** or **B** to indicate which statement is more general.

Sample Sentences
A. They played hide-and-seek.
B. They played a game.

Item 1: A. She bought a belt.
B. She bought an article of clothing.

Item 2: A. He runs every morning.
B. Ted Baxter runs every morning.

Item 3: A. She observed the animals.
B. She observed the monkeys.

Item 4: A. They observed animals.
B. Three children observed animals.

Item 5: A. Six hungry ducklings followed their mother.
B. Six ducklings followed their mother.

Item 6: A. We visited Lisa and Bill.
B. We visited them.

Part F

- The simplest argument you can construct has three parts. The first two parts are the evidence. The last part is the conclusion.

- Here's an example:

> **Evidence:** **All birds have feathers.**
> **A sora is a bird.**
> **Conclusion:** **Therefore, a sora has feathers.**

Part G | For each item, write the conclusion that follows from the evidence.

Item 1: All gasoline engines have exhaust manifolds.
VMX engines are gasoline engines.

[   ] .

Item 2: Doris is more insidious than Clara.
Clara is more insidious than Denny.

[   ] .

Item 3: The magazine article is more terse than the newspaper article.
The newspaper article is more terse than the record.

[   ] .

Part H | Follow the outline diagram to describe the problem with each argument.

Outline diagram

Argument __ concludes that _____ _____ ;	however, that conclusion does not follow from the evidence.
	The correct conclusion is that _____ .

Sample Argument

Argument A
All squirrels are mammals.
All mammals have lungs.
THEREFORE, all squirrels have tails.

Argument A concludes that **all squirrels have tails;** however, that conclusion does not follow from the evidence. The correct conclusion is that **all squirrels have lungs.**

Argument 1: Mr. Jackson loves legumes.
Peas are legumes.
Therefore, peas love Mr. Jackson.

Argument 2: All guide dogs are well trained.
Our dog is a guide dog.
Therefore, our dog never barks.

Lesson 2

Part A | Write the letter of the more specific statement.

Item 1: A. They learned things.
          B. They learned to read hard words.

Item 2: A. Rita loved to read novels.
          B. Rita loved to read things.

Item 3: A. Some people make a lot of noise.
          B. Some babies make a lot of noise.

Part B | For each item, construct a sentence that is more specific than either sentence shown by using parts of those sentences.

Sample Argument
A. The man in the gray coat had some money.
B. He had $34.25.

1. A. They went to Jim Franklin's house.
   B. Three boys went to his house.

2. A. The car belongs to the people who live across the street.
   B. The car with a flat tire belongs to neighbors.

3. A. She cleaned Amy's teeth.
   B. The dental hygienist cleaned them.

4. A. They are reptiles with no legs.
   B. Snakes are animals with no legs.

Part C | Test each word to see if it's a noun. If it is a noun, write the word **one** or **some** in front of it.

1. slowly
2. happy
3. dream
4. stories
5. not
6. willing
7. turkey
8. lonely
9. stupid
10. racket

| For each item, write the conclusion that follows from the evidence.

Item 1: Sally is demurer than Fran.
Fran is demurer than Hilda.

Item 2: Melvin is more calumnious than Wanda.
Wanda is more calumnious than Mr. Briggs.

Item 3: A hexagon has more sides than a rectangle.
A rectangle has more sides than a triangle.

Part E | For each item, follow the outline diagram to tell about another possibility.

Item 1

Irma lives two blocks from the ocean. One day, she saw her brother coming home. He was soaking wet. The sky was dark in the distance, and the streets were wet. Irma said to herself, "My brother got caught in the rain."

Item 2

Dan did not see Ellen over the summer. When school let out in the spring, she had dark brown hair and light skin. In the fall, she had very dark skin and blonde hair. Dan said, "Ellen must have bleached her hair to make it blonde."

Item 3

Mr. Jackson called his wife. He indicated that he would be home late because he had to finish important work at the office. Mrs. Jackson could hear people laughing in the background. She said to herself, "He's not working. He's having a party."

Outline diagram

| ___[Name]___ concluded that _____ _____. | ✗ | Another possibility is that _____ _____. |

Follow the outline diagram to tell what is wrong with Lisa's decision.

Henry's requirements

1. The jacket must cost less than $200.
2. The jacket must be washable.
3. The jacket must offer superior protection against the cold.
4. The jacket must weigh no more than 4 pounds.

Why Lisa bought the Windblaster

Henry wanted a jacket that costs less than $200, and Windblaster certainly meets that requirement. It costs only $187.99. Henry also wanted a jacket that offers superior protection against the cold. Windblaster is rated as having superior protection. And Windblaster is very light. It weighs only 3 pounds 2 ounces. Weight is important to Henry, and he wanted a jacket that weighs 4 pounds or less. So I don't see how he could possibly go wrong with Windblaster.

Facts

Jacket	Stormblaster	Windblaster	Leader	King Kold	Wilderness
Price	$179.00	$187.99	$156.00	$206.00	$187.00
Weight	4 lb.	3 lb. 2 oz.	2 lb. 8 oz.	3 lb. 7 oz.	4 lb. 3 oz.
Protection against cold	superior	superior	good	superior	superior
Cleaning	washable	dry clean only	washable	washable	washable

Outline diagram

The jacket that Lisa selected does not meet all of Henry's requirements.

Henry wants _____ _____ _____ ; however, Windblaster _____ _____ .

Lisa should have selected _____ . = [Tell why.]

Part G | The things that the older gentleman says in the following passage are not complete sentences. Write a complete sentence for each response that is not a sentence.

Passage

Mary had just moved into town. As she was waiting for a bus, she struck up a conversation with an older gentleman.

1. Mary: Where's a good place to buy light fixtures?
   Older gentleman: Denny's Hardware.

2. Mary: Where is Denny's Hardware?
   Older gentleman: Two blocks down the street.

3. Mary: I also need to connect my phone. Where is the phone office?
   Older gentleman: Way on the other side of town.

4. Mary: Well, maybe I can call them. Which bus should I take to get downtown?
   Older gentleman: Number four.

Lesson 3

Part A | Write **N** if the sentence ends with a noun.

1. They went north.
2. They worked rapidly.
3. They asked questions.
4. They studied subjects.
5. They looked worried.
6. They read about characters.

7. It was noisy.
8. It was made of granite.
9. They drank lots of fluids.
10. It was evaporating.
11. They were managers.
12. The movie was thrilling.

Part B | For each item, follow the outline diagram to tell about another possibility.

Item 1

Fred is a very sloppy person. The other day, Ann saw him as he was returning to the office from lunch. She noticed that he had an egg stain on his shirt. She concluded that Fred had eaten eggs for lunch.

Item 2

Mr. Franklin instructed his secretary to file a report on teenage crime in England. Later, when his secretary was out of the office, Mr. Franklin tried to find the report. He looked through the **Ts** in her file cabinet to see if he could find the report under **teenage** or **teens.** He didn't find it. Then he looked under **C** for **crime,** and he couldn't find it. He concluded that she had lost the report.

Item 3

Mrs. Rodriguez put her two-year-old child in the high chair and gave her a glass of milk. Then she let the cat in and got the paper. When she came back, the cat was lapping up spilled milk on the floor. Mrs. Rodriguez concluded that the child had spilled her milk.

Outline diagram

Part C | Follow the outline diagram to write about the jacket that meets all of Mr. Taylor's requirements.

Mr. Taylor's requirements

1. The jacket must be washable.
2. The jacket must offer superior protection against the cold.
3. The jacket must weigh no more than 4 pounds.

Facts

Jacket	Hiker	Windblaster	Leader	King Kold	Wilderness
Price	$210.00	$187.99	$156.00	$206.00	$187.00
Weight	4 lb.	3 lb. 2 oz.	2 lb. 8 oz.	3 lb. 7 oz.	4 lb. 3 oz.
Protection against cold	good	superior	good	superior	superior
Cleaning	washable	dry clean only	washable	washable	washable

Outline diagram

_____ is the jacket that meets all of Mr. Taylor's requirements.

Requirement 1 rules out _____.
[Tell why.]

Requirement 2 rules out _____.
[Tell why.]

Requirement 3 rules out _____.
[Tell why.]

The only remaining choice is _____.

Part D For each item, construct a sentence that is more specific than the other sentences by using the most specific first part and the most specific second part of the three sentences.

1. A. A young man studied history.

   B. A young person studied a subject.

   C. A male studied Canadian history.

2. A. The store was in a large city on the east coast of the U.S.

   B. The structure was in a large city.

   C. The building was in New York City.

3. A. Judge Mason asked about their activities on the night of April 5.

   B. The judge asked about their activities.

   C. He asked about the activities of Billy and Bobby Taylor on the night of April 5.

4. A. Nearly all female spiders are larger than them.

   B. Many of them are larger than male spiders.

   C. They are larger than males.

Part E

Each item presents evidence. You'll write the conclusion. Don't copy the arguments. Just write the conclusions.

Item 1: All clay pots are fragile.
Raku pots are clay pots.

[   ] .

Item 2: All birds with red eyes gather food during the day.
A snail kite is a red-eyed bird.

[   ] .

Item 3: Trees don't grow where the ground never thaws.
The ground never thaws in northern Alaska.

[   ] .

Lesson

| Write **N** if the sentence ends with a noun.

1. They had awkward relationships.
2. They were energetic.
3. They were in columns.
4. They worked hard.
5. They looked into other possibilities.
6. Our vacation was delayed.
7. They had a long delay.
8. Those animals are reptiles.
9. They looked disgusted.
10. They were following dolphins.
11. They were alert.
12. They were sinking.
13. They were new activities.

For each item, follow the outline diagram to tell about another possibility.

Item 1

Mr. Franklin instructed his secretary to file a report on wheat farming in the Midwest. Later, she told him that the report was filed. A week later, he looked under M for Midwest and did not find it. He concluded that she probably had not filed the report yet.

Item 2

Mr. Kennedy discovered that when he ate some foods, he broke out in a rash. Whenever he ate a ham sandwich with mustard and tomatoes or a hamburger with mustard and lettuce, he got a rash. These were the only sandwiches he ever ate. He concluded that he must be allergic to mustard.

Item 3

Juan saw a young woman in a hospital. She was wearing a white outfit, and she was carrying a clipboard. Two other young women were walking with her. Both wore nurse's caps. Juan concluded that the young woman carrying the clipboard was also a nurse.

Outline diagram

For each item, follow the outline diagram to support or discredit the rules given.

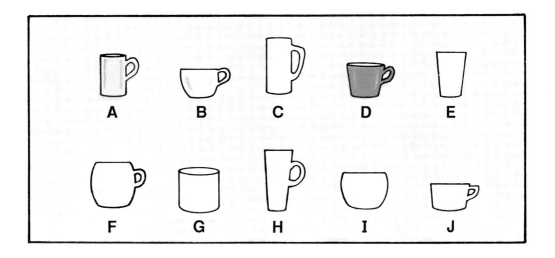

Rule 1: All of the cups have handles.

Item 1: Jenny examined cups in this order: A, B, C, F, H.

Item 2: Linda examined cups in this order: F, G, H, D, E.

Rule 2: Some of the cups are shaped like a cylinder.

Item 3: Tom examined cups in this order: A, B, C, D, E.

Item 4: Mike examined cups in this order: B, D, F, H, J.

Rule 3: All of the cups are white.

Item 5: Henry examined cups in this order: E, I, H, D, B, A.

Item 6: Ginger examined cups in this order: B, C, E, G, I.

Outline diagram

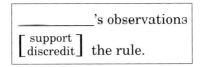

- A conclusion of a proper argument can never be **more general** than the evidence that leads to the conclusion.

- Here is evidence for an argument:

  Children like to play tag.
  Tag is an active game.

- Here is a conclusion that is more general than the evidence:

  Therefore, children like all active games.

- The conclusion is not acceptable because it is more general than the corresponding evidence. The evidence in this argument does not lead to any proper conclusions.

Part E For each argument, indicate whether the conclusion is **more specific** than the evidence or **more general** than the evidence.

Argument 1: Dan loves the smell of roses.
Roses are flowers with thorns.
Therefore, Dan loves the smell of all flowers with thorns.

Argument 2: All arguments have a conclusion.
Argument 2 is an argument.
Therefore, argument 2 has a conclusion.

Argument 3: All the residents of Homer Island are excellent fishermen.
Jane Carter is a resident of Homer Island.
Therefore, Jane Carter is an excellent fisherman.

Argument 4: The students at Fenger School do well in all subjects.
Music is a subject.
Therefore, the students at Fenger School do well in music.

Argument 5: Grace Brown is the best bike rider I know.
Grace lives on Homer Island.
Therefore, all the girls on Homer Island must be excellent bike riders.

Argument 6: Ted did poorly in math.
Math is an academic subject.
Therefore, Ted must have done poorly in all academic subjects.

Part F | Each item presents evidence. You'll write the conclusion. Don't copy the arguments. Just write the conclusions.

Item 1:   All people from Polk County talk a lot.
Carol Hillary is from Polk County.

.

Item 2:   All mammals have a tongue.
A whale is a mammal.

.

Item 3:   All periodicals are published regularly.
The *Weekly Digest* is a periodical.

.

Item 4:   All people who own a business make decisions.
Mr. Harrison owns a business.

.

Part G | For each item, use parts of the sentences to construct a sentence that is more specific than the other sentences.

1. A. He learned to drive a bus.

    B. Hector learned to drive a vehicle.

    C. The man learned to drive a long bus.

2. A. It caused a delay in the delivery.

    B. The weather caused a delay in the mail delivery.

    C. The snowstorm caused the delay.

Lesson 5

- You've learned that nouns name things that can be counted or pointed to.

- Any nouns in a sentence may be replaced with **pronouns. Pronouns are more general words than nouns.**

- Here's a sentence that ends with a noun:

    Tom went with his friends.

- You can replace the words **his friends** with a pronoun:

    Tom went with them.

- Here's another sentence that ends with a noun:

    Tom went to the store.

- You can replace the words **the store** with a pronoun:

    Tom went to it.

- Remember, a pronoun is a **more general word** that **replaces a noun.** It's more general because it can be used to refer to more things than the noun refers to.

Part B | The last two words in each sentence are an adjective and a noun. Replace that part with a pronoun that makes sense.

1. John walked with his cane.

2. The engine of the train pulled 15 cars.

3. Don had an argument with his sister.

4. Frank drank cold water.

5. Mr. Jackson fixed large hamburgers.

6. Mrs. Taylor was proud of her son.

For each argument, indicate whether the conclusion is **more general** or **more specific** than the evidence.

Argument 1: Tim has expensive shoes.
Shoes are articles of clothing.
Therefore, Tim must have other expensive articles of clothing.

Argument 2: Rita hates rats.
Rats are rodents.
Therefore, Rita must hate all rodents.

Argument 3: Hank loves all rodents.
Squirrels are rodents.
Therefore, Hank loves squirrels.

Argument 4: All mammals hold their breath under water.
Whales are mammals.
Therefore, whales hold their breath under water.

Argument 5: Thistles are plants that have thorns.
Thistles are weeds.
Therefore, all plants that have thorns are weeds.

Argument 6: They love to eat shrimp.
Shrimp are sea animals.
Therefore, they love to eat all sea animals.

Part D | For each item, follow the outline diagram to support or discredit the rule given.

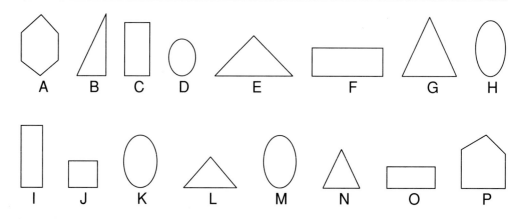

Rule 1: All of the figures have straight sides.

Item 1: Mark examined figures in this order: A, B, C, D, I, J, K, L.

Item 2: Susan examined figures in this order: P, O, N, G, F, E, B.

Rule 2: Some of the figures have more than four sides.

Item 3: Alex examined figures in this order: A, B, C, D, M, N, O, P.

Item 4: Anne examined figures in this order: B, D, E, G, H, I.

Rule 3: None of the figures have five sides.

Item 5: Andy examined figures in this order: A, B, C, D, E, F, G, H.

Item 6: Andrea examined figures in this order: P, O, N, M, L, K, J, I.

Outline diagram

> _____'s observations
>
> $\begin{bmatrix} \text{support} \\ \text{discredit} \end{bmatrix}$ the rule.

| | Follow the outline diagram to tell about the **best** choice for a vacation spot. |

Smith family's vacation requirements

1. They don't want to travel to a resort that is more than 800 miles away.
2. The resort they stay at can't be more than 30 miles from a body of water. Also, it can't be more than 20 miles from the mountains.
3. The resort they stay at can't cost more than $95 a day.
4. The resort must have hiking trails, horses and a swimming pool or lake.
5. The unit they stay in must have 2 bedrooms.

Facts

Resorts	Sleepy Valley	Dude Plus Ranch	Fun Town	Outback Village
Distance from home	1330 miles	590 miles	738 miles	370 miles
Setting	26 miles from Stoner's Peak 18 miles from the ocean	12 miles from Mt. Tunis on Swift River and Stallion Lake	20 miles from Mt. Lincoln 42 miles from Dover Lake	6 miles from Mt. Taylor 600 feet from Loner Lake
Price	$85 a day	$100 a day	$100 a day	$68 a day
Available activities	hiking horseback riding swimming pool tennis	horseback riding hiking swimming (lake or river)	carnival rides hiking olympic-size pool tennis	hiking swimming (lake)
Accommodations	2-bedroom unit	2-bedroom unit	2-bedroom unit	1-bedroom units only

Outline diagram

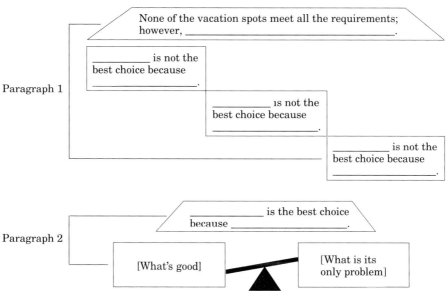

None of the vacation spots meet all the requirements; however, _____.

Paragraph 1

_____ is not the best choice because _____.

_____ is not the best choice because _____.

_____ is not the best choice because _____.

Paragraph 2

_____ is the best choice because _____.

[What's good]

[What is its only problem]

Part F | Write the letter of the sentence that is more specific.

Item 1: A. He likes tuna fish.
B. Mitch likes tuna fish.

Item 2: A. Ann broke the bicycle part.
B. Ann broke the bicycle sprocket.

Item 3: A. The students gathered around a reference book.
B. The students gathered around an atlas.

Part G | Write the conclusion for each item.

Item 1: All crustaceans have a hard shell.
A lobster is a crustacean.

.

Item 2: All spiders have more than six legs.
A black widow is a spider.

.

Item 3: All machines have moving parts.
A bicycle is a machine.

.

Lesson 6

- Pronouns are more general words that replace nouns.
- Here's a sentence that ends with a pronoun:

  We watched **them.**

- If we replace the word **them** with two words that make sense, those words will be an adjective and a noun.
- Here is a list of word pairs that make sense:

  We watched **five dogs.**
  We watched **those children.**
  We watched **our neighbors.**
  We watched **flying birds.**
  We watched **other movies.**

- For all of the examples, the last word is a noun. The word just before it is an **adjective.** **Adjectives** are words that make nouns more specific by telling **what kind** or **how many.**

If a sentence ends with a noun, write **N.** If a sentence ends with a pronoun, replace the pronoun with two words that make sense, and label the parts of speech for those words.

1. They were amazed by it.
2. They loved entertainment.
3. Nancy reads them.
4. Chris almost got hit by it.
5. Kay fixed a delicious meal.
6. We overheard their entire conversation.
7. Mr. Raymond was disappointed when he heard it.
8. Greg hated to go places with her.
9. Our favorite program was a big hit.
10. Everybody on the team was happy after they won it.

Part C

> **Facts**
>
> - When you discredit a rule, you show that it is false.
> - If a rule tells about **all,** you can show that the rule is false by finding **one thing** that does not fit the rule.

Part D

Rule: All black cats have paws with eight claws.

Item 1: To discredit the rule, you would examine cats. What kind of cats would you examine?

Item 2: Why wouldn't you examine yellow cats?

Item 3: If all of the cats you examine have paws with eight claws, your observations would support the rule.

Item 4: To discredit the rule, you would have to find at least one black cat that did not have eight claws.

Part E | Write an answer for each item.

Rule: It is always hotter in the afternoon than it is in the morning.

Item 1: To discredit the rule, you would look at particular times of day. Which times?

Item 2: Why wouldn't you examine evenings?

Item 3: If the rule is true, how many of the days you examine would be warmer in the morning than in the afternoon?

Item 4: To discredit the rule, you would have to observe days in which the afternoon is not warmer than the morning. How many of those days would you have to observe?

Item 5: Let's say that you observed 120 days and discovered 1 day that had a high temperature in the morning of 66° and a high temperature in the afternoon of 66°. What could you conclude about the rule?

Follow the outline diagram to describe the problem with the arguments.

Argument 1: Dan loves the smell of roses.
Roses are flowers with thorns.
Therefore, Dan loves the smell of all flowers with thorns.

Argument 2: Rita hates rats.
Rats are rodents.
Therefore, Rita must hate all rodents.

Argument 3: Jane Carter is an excellent fisherman.
Jane Carter is a resident of Homer Island.
Therefore, all the residents of Homer Island are excellent fishermen.

Outline diagram

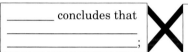

| _____ concludes that _____ _____ ; | X | however, the conclusion is more general than the evidence. Evidence about [specific category] cannot lead to a proper conclusion about [general category]. |

Part G

Write the one-word response for each item. Then write the full-sentence answer for each question.

1. A. How many days are in a week?
    B. What is five plus two?

2. A. The morning sun is in which direction?
    B. Which direction is the opposite of west?

Part H | Write sentences for all the responses that are not complete sentences.

1. Mother: When will you work on your homework?
   Joe: This evening.

2. Mother: I thought you told Mark that you would go with him to the art exhibit.
   Joe: I forgot all about that.

3. Mother: So, what are you going to do?
   Joe: Work on my homework now.

4. Mother: Will you be able to finish it before dinner?
   Joe: Perhaps.

Part I | Use the underlined parts to write a sentence that is more specific than the sentences that are shown.

1. A. Some butterflies have delicate wings with beautiful designs.

   B. Monarch butterflies have wings.

2. A. They watched the last game of the playoffs.

   B. Helen, Bill and Tina watched a sporting event.

Lesson 7

Part A

If a sentence ends with a noun, write **N.** If a sentence ends with a pronoun, replace the pronoun with two words that make sense, and label the parts of speech for those words.

1. They were proud of it.

2. Last night we had pizza for dinner.

3. The workers lost their nerve.

4. Their trees were full of them.

5. The judge warned her.

Part B

Follow the outline diagram to write about the arguments that are not proper.

Argument 1: Mr. Hayes could paint all types of wooden buildings.
Our garage is a wooden building.
Therefore, Mr. Hayes could paint our garage.

Argument 2: Turtles hold their breath under water.
Turtles are marine animals.
Therefore, all marine animals hold their breath under water.

Argument 3: They love to eat shrimp.
Shrimp are marine animals.
Therefore, they love to eat all marine animals.

Argument 4: All mammals are warm blooded.
Whales are mammals.
Therefore, whales are warm blooded.

Outline diagram

| _____ concludes that _____ _____ ; | ✕ | however, the conclusion is more _____ _____. Evidence about _____ cannot _____ _____ . |

Rule: No rocks float in water.

Item 1: To discredit the rule, you would examine objects in water. What kind of objects?

Item 2: Why wouldn't you examine wood?

Item 3: If the rule is true, how many of the rocks you examine would sink?

Item 4: To discredit the rule, you have to find rocks that did not sink in water. How many rocks would you have to find?

Item 5: If you examined 180 rocks and discovered that they all sank, would your observations support the rule or discredit it?

Part D

- When you compare two things, you should use parallel words to refer to each thing you're comparing.

- Here's a sentence that uses parallel words:

  The mail was delivered faster to Chicago than to New York.

- The parallel parts are **to Chicago** and **to New York.**

- Here's a sentence that does not have complete parallel wording:

  The mail was delivered faster to Chicago than New York.

- When you write carefully, you should make the wording as parallel as you can to express the intended meaning.

Sample Sentence   The man worked harder than the boy.

Write a parallel sentence for each item.

1. The dogs ran faster than the children.
2. Wayne suffered more from the cold than the wind.
3. They put more gas in the tractor than the truck.
4. The horse weighed more than the cow.
5. Diane crawls faster than Frances.
6. The wind blew faster from the west than the north.

Independent Work

Write the conclusion for each argument.

Item 1: All the families who live on Oak Street have at least two cars.
The DeMet family lives on Oak Street.

.

Item 2: Dogs have more trouble sleeping when the moon is full.
The moon will be full tonight.

.

Item 3: Heavy land animals have thick leg bones.
The rhinoceros is a heavy land animal.

.

Follow the outline diagram to explain the problem with the argument.

Here's what Mary's Aunt Liz said:

When Mary left for school this morning, she did not have a skinned-up knee. Mary came home from school with a skinned-up knee. Therefore, she must have skinned her knee on the school playground.

Outline diagram

Part A | Write a parallel sentence for each item.

1. The heater made more noise than the radio.

2. The watch kept better time than the clock.

3. The temperature was higher in the morning than the afternoon.

4. They would rather go with Ted than Margaret.

5. My uncle drives faster than my mother.

6. The wallpaper looks prettier in yellow than orange.

Part B

- You've worked with **adjectives.** Those are words that come before nouns and that make nouns more specific. **Adjectives** tell **what kind** or **how many.**

- Here is a sentence that ends with an adjective:

  They were tired.

- The word **tired** is an adjective.

- You can show it's an adjective by writing a noun after it:

  They were **tired workers.**

Part C | Use two or three words to rewrite the ending of each sentence so it ends with a noun. Then label the parts of speech for the new ending of the sentence.

1. His daughter was lovely.

2. The dictionary is useful.

3. Cabbage is nutritious.

4. A hurricane is powerful.

5. Jets are fast.

Sample Sentence

If [something happens], Marvin could be hit by a car.

For each item, write a sentence that explains something that could happen. Remember the comma.

1. If [something happens], Joe will not be in school tomorrow.
2. If [something happens], we'll get soaked.
3. If [something happens], the plants will die.
4. If [something happens], our electricity will go off.

Independent Work

Part E

If an argument has a conclusion that is more general than the evidence, follow the outline diagram to write about the argument.

Argument 1: All writing instruments may be used to create words.
All pens are writing instruments.
Therefore, all pens may be used to create words.

Argument 2: All pens write with ink.
All pens are writing instruments.
Therefore, all writing instruments write with ink.

Outline diagram

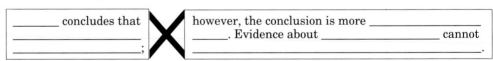

| _____ concludes that _____ _____ ; | | however, the conclusion is more _____ _____. Evidence about _____ cannot _____ . |

| For each argument, write the conclusion.

Argument 1: Penguins are birds.
Birds have feathers.

[   ] .

Argument 2: My neighbors are noisy people.
Noisy people are annoying.

[   ] .

Argument 3: Mini loves expensive things.
Railroad locomotives are expensive things.

[   ] .

Lesson 9

Part A | For each item, follow the outline diagram to tell about another possibility.

Item 1

Dale and Fran were at a meeting. Dale had the program that told about the things that were to happen at the meeting. Fran asked him when they would discuss building the Community Center. Dale looked at the program for a few moments. Then he blinked and said that he couldn't see well enough to read the program. He handed the program to Fran. She quickly found the item she was looking for. Fran concluded that Dale needed glasses.

Item 2

Jerry saw a picture of Hilda at a lake. The sun was behind her, near the horizon. Jerry concluded that the picture was taken early in the morning.

Outline diagram

Part B

- Some sentences that compare do not need wording that is perfectly parallel. In fact, perfectly parallel wording sometimes makes a silly meaning.

- Here's a sentence:

    Linda lifted more than the barbells.

- If we make the sentence parallel, it has a silly meaning:

    Linda lifted more than the barbells lifted.

- The meaning is silly because barbells don't lift.

Write the number of each sentence that would have a silly meaning if you rewrote it. Then rewrite the other sentences so that they are parallel.

1. Tina painted faster than her father.
2. Freddie ate less than the rest of the students.
3. Freddie ate less than a plateful.
4. Soo Lin lost more than ten dollars.
5. She walked faster to the store than the school.
6. Marie walked more than a mile.
7. More rain fell in the morning than the evening.
8. The lily smelled better than the rose.

Part D | Follow the outline diagram to write a paragraph about what would discredit the rule.

Rule: All black cats have paws with eight claws.

Outline diagram

To test the rule, you could examine _____ _____.

If _____ _____, the evidence would discredit the rule.

If _____ _____, the evidence would not discredit the rule.

Part E | For each item, write a sentence that explains something that could happen. Remember the comma.

1. If [something happens], your bike will get a flat tire.
2. If [something happens], Jennifer will lose a lot of weight.
3. If [something happens], Denny will not go to the same school next year.

Part F | For each item, indicate the letter of the more general sentence.

Item 1: A. Maggie bought lots of tomatoes.
B. Maggie bought lots of groceries.

Item 2: A. Andrew hated outdoor activities.
B. Andrew hated hiking in the woods.

Item 3: A. The leaves on apple trees produce oxygen.
B. Green leaves produce oxygen.

Part G | Follow the outline diagram to write about the problem with the argument.

Argument: Alice's pet is a mammal.
A cat is a mammal.
Therefore, Alice's pet is a cat.

Outline diagram

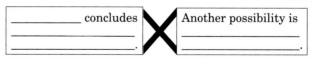

Lesson 10 – Test 1

Part A | For each argument, write the conclusion.

Argument 1: Seeds with two halves are dicot seeds.
A bean is a seed that has two parts.

[   ] .

Argument 2: All true ferns have spores.
Mosses do not have spores.

[   ] .

Argument 3: Mammals are warm blooded.
Bats are mammals.

[   ] .

Argument 4: All arguments present evidence.
Item 2 is an argument.

[   ] .

Part B | Follow the outline diagram to write about the problem with the argument.

Argument: Donna does exercises every day.
Sit-ups and push-ups are exercises.
Therefore, when Donna exercises, she does sit-ups and push-ups.

Outline diagram

	Another possibility __
	_____
	_____ .

Part C | Rewrite every sentence so it is as parallel as possible. After each rewritten sentence write **silly** if it has a silly meaning.

1. She liked more than the cake.
2. The pitcher threw more balls than the catcher.
3. The typewriter costs less than the computer.
4. She dropped more than the eggs.
5. The dog ran more slowly than the cat.

Part D | Write the part of speech for the last word of each sentence. If the sentence does not end with a noun, write an ending that has one or two adjectives and a noun. Write letters to show the parts of speech of the new ending.

1. Hard work develops them.
2. Whales are large.
3. Our dog kept following it.
4. I disagree with her arguments.

Write whether each boy's observations support the rule or discredit the rule. If the observations discredit the rule, show the objects the boy would have observed until he first knew that the rule had been discredited.

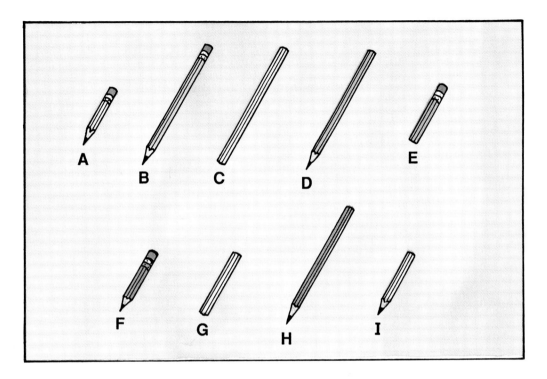

Rule: All short pencils have erasers.

Item 1:   Greg examined pencils in this order: A, B, C, D, E, F.

Item 2:   Leo examined pencils in this order: A, B, C, F, G, H, I.

Outline diagram

_____'s observations

$\begin{bmatrix} \text{support} \\ \text{discredit} \end{bmatrix}$ the rule.

Part A | For each item, write the letter that shows the part of speech for the last word. If the last word is not a noun, rewrite the ending using one or two adjectives and a noun. Label the parts of speech for the new ending.

1. Most warehouses are large.

2. Everybody was angry about her remarks.

3. We tried to keep up with her.

4. Last winter was cold.

5. The judge announced his decision.

6. The wires were tangled around it.

7. Redwoods are gigantic.

8. The noise disturbed them.

Part B | Write about the arguments that do not have proper conclusions.

Argument 1:   Jake does well in math.
Math is an academic subject.
Therefore, Jake does well in all academic subjects.

Argument 2:   A conclusion is a sentence.
All sentences are made up of words.
Therefore, a conclusion is made up of words.

Argument 3:   Elisa is shy around strangers.
Elisa is not a leader.
Therefore, everybody who is shy around strangers is not a leader.

Argument 4:   I have a dog named George.
George barks a lot.
Therefore, everybody named George must bark a lot.

Outline diagram

_____	however, _____
_____	_____
_____;	_____.

Follow the outline diagram to describe how you would test the rule.

Rule: The high temperature in the morning is always different from the high temperature in the afternoon.

Outline diagram

To test the rule, you could _____
_____.

If _____
_____,
the evidence would
discredit the rule.

If _____
_____,
the evidence would
not discredit the rule.

Independent Work

Part D | Use the appropriate outline diagram to tell about each argument.

1. Janice was the last person in the house. After she left, the water was running in the bathroom. She must have been in the bathroom and forgot to turn off the water.

2. *Here's what Al said:* I have concluded that all hounds howl early in the morning. I drew this conclusion because Jed Wilcox has hounds, and they're always howling early in the morning.

Outline diagrams

_____
_____
_____;

however, the conclusion _____
_____. Evidence about _____
_____.

_____
_____
_____.

Another possibility
_____
_____.

Rewrite all the sentences so they are parallel. Make sure they don't have a silly meaning.

1. They planted more in the side yard than the garden.
2. The gardener carried more tools than Martha.
3. My brother eats a lot more than my father.
4. The flowers looked better on the table than the counter.
5. Our neighbors make a lot more noise than we.

Part A | Follow the outline diagram to describe how you would test the rule.

Rule: All rocks sink in water.

Outline diagram

To test the rule, you could _____ _____.

If _____ _____, the evidence would discredit the rule.

If _____ _____, the evidence would not discredit the rule.

Part B

- A **verb** is an important part of speech.
- All sentences have a verb.
- The verb may be one word or more than one word.
- Here is a sentence with a one-word verb:
    She walked fast.
- Here is a sentence with a two-word verb:
    She was walking fast.
- Here is a sentence with a three-word verb:
    She has been walking fast.
- The actor in the sentences above is **she.** The verb in the sentences tells what she **did** or **was doing.**
- Some verbs tell what the actor **has** or **is:**
    She has black hair.
    She is a good student.
- The verb does two important things in the sentence. It usually tells whether there's **one actor** or **more than one actor.** The verb also indicates whether the sentence refers to the **past,** to the **present** time, or to **future** possibilities.

Part C Write **X, Y** or **Z** to indicate what you know about the number of actors in each sentence.

X = one actor
Y = more than one actor
Z = one actor or more than one actor

Sample Sentences

	Actor(s)	Verb	Other words
A.		ran	.
B.		is talking	.

	Actor(s)	Verb	Other words
1.		looks	.
2.		were riding	.
3.		will go	.
4.		is wondering	.
5.		bought	.
6.		see	.
7.		stops	.

Part D Rewrite every sentence so it is as parallel as possible. Write **silly** after each rewritten sentence that has a silly meaning.

1. She painted more than the floor.
2. She threw more than a dozen stones.
3. Tom read more books than his sister.
4. Rosa read more than the magazines.
5. She collected less than her sisters.
6. Tigers sleep longer than dogs.

Part E For each item, follow the outline diagram to tell about another possibility.

Item 1

Doris saw a man stop his car on the side of the road, jump out of the car with his hands waving this way and that, and run into a field. He stood there for some time, rubbing his arm and looking at it. Then he walked back to his car cautiously, carrying a stick that he found in the field. Doris said to herself, "That man is either drunk or crazy."

Item 2

Sarah looked at a picture of Lois. The picture showed Lois standing next to a sign that said, "Welcome to Freemont, Vermont." The date that was stamped on the back of the photo was June 11. Sarah concluded that Lois had been in Vermont in June.

Outline diagram

Part F Follow the appropriate outline diagram to explain the proper conclusion for each argument.

Argument 1: All whales are mammals.
All mammals have lungs.
Therefore, all mammals are warm blooded.

Argument 2: Gail does well in all academic subjects.
Writing is an academic subject.
Therefore, Gail loves to write.

Argument 3: Bikes are vehicles with two wheels.
All vehicles with two wheels must be balanced.
Therefore, motorcycles must be balanced.

Outline diagrams

Argument __ concludes that _____ _____ ;	✕	however, that conclusion does not follow from the evidence. The correction conclusion is: ___ _____ .

Argument __ concludes that _____ _____ ;	✕	Another possibility is that _____ _____ .

Part G Write the letter that shows the part of speech for the last word in each sentence. If the last word is not a noun, rewrite the ending so it has one or two adjectives and a noun.

1. We spent a long time looking at it.
2. Trout are tasty.
3. Roger was friendly.
4. Our biggest concern was with the weather.
5. Jill kept suggesting bad ideas.
6. Nobody liked him.

Lesson 13

Part A

For each item, write the letter that shows the part of speech for the last word. If the last word is not a noun, rewrite the ending using one or two adjectives and a noun. Label the parts of speech for the new ending.

1. My mother baked cookies.

2. I became sick.

3. Good screwdrivers are sturdy.

4. The boys stared at them.

Part B

Sample Sentences

Linda wore more than the model in the picture.

Silly meaning:
The sentence indicates that Linda wore the model in the picture.

Perfectly parallel sentence:
Linda wore more than the model in the picture wore.

For each item, write a sentence that indicates the silly meaning.

1. She bought more at the market than the department store.

> **Sentence ___ indicates that she bought ____**
> [silly meaning]
> _____ .

2. Chickens lay more eggs than turtles.

> **Sentence ___ indicates that chickens lay ___**
> [silly meaning]
> _____ .

3. Dan ate a lot more than his dog.

4. Vickie lifted more than Terry.

5. Brenda found more ugly things than Ann.

6. The dog dug up more things than the cat.

- The verb words in a sentence indicate whether the sentence tells about the past, the present or the future.

Sample Sentences

A. The boys are walking.

B. The boys went on a walk.

C. The boys will go on a walk.

Part D Write **past, present** or **future** to tell about each sentence.

1. Paul stands in the room.
2. We are watching an interesting program.
3. The girls are telling secrets to each other.
4. The sailboat will tip over.
5. That fish smells rotten.
6. They bought a lot of groceries.
7. Our mother is very busy this morning.
8. The workers were tired.
9. The train will make four stops.
10. Bees buzzed the flowers.

You go to a strange land that has strange creatures. A book about the land has rules about the creatures that you'll see.

Here are the rules:

1. All creatures with an eye have a tail.
2. All creatures with a tail have an eye.
3. All creatures with a pointed top have eyelashes.
4. All creatures with eyelashes have a pointed top.
5. All creatures with a pointed top have an eye.
6. All creatures with an eye have a pointed top.

You have trouble imagining what those creatures look like. So you examine six creatures. When you compare them to the rules, you find that the evidence discredits some of the rules.

Answer these questions.

Questions

1. Which of the creatures you examined does rule 1 tell about?
2. Which of the creatures discredits rule 1?
3. Why does that creature discredit the rule?

4. Which of the creatures you examined does rule 2 tell about?
5. Which of the creatures discredits rule 2?

6. Which of the creatures you examined does rule 3 tell about?
7. Which of the creatures discredits rule 3?
8. Why does that creature discredit the rule?

9. Which of the creatures you examined does rule 4 tell about?
10. Which of the creatures discredits rule 4?

11. Which of the creatures you examined does rule 5 tell about?
12. Which of the creatures discredits the rule?

13. Which of the creatures you examined does rule 6 tell about?
14. Which of the creatures discredits rule 6?
15. Why does that creature discredit the rule?

Here are the creatures

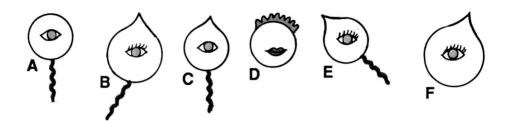

Independent Work

Part F

Rewrite each sentence in part B so it is parallel and does not have a silly meaning.

Part G

If the argument has a conclusion that is more general than the evidence, explain the problem with the argument. If the conclusion is not more general than the evidence, don't write anything.

Argument 1: Animals with tails are not humans.
Goldfish have tails.
Therefore, goldfish are not humans.

Argument 2: Goldfish have tails.
Goldfish are creatures that live in water.
Therefore, all creatures that live in water have tails.

Argument 3: Jan's car is a Bumpo.
Jan's car breaks down a lot.
Therefore, all Bumpos break down a lot.

Outline diagram

_____	however, the conclusion is more general _____
_____	_____. Evidence about _____
_____;	_____.

Part A Follow the outline diagram to write about each sentence that has a silly meaning.

1. John ate less than two hamburgers.
2. In the last game, the Tigers scored more than three touchdowns.
3. The mouse ate more than the cat.
4. Joey bought more than his cousin Marvin.
5. Angela ran farther than five miles.
6. Sidney jumped higher than his father.
7. Margaret slept longer than eight hours.

Outline diagram

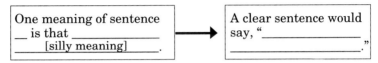

Part B For each sentence, write **X, Y** or **Z** to indicate the number of actors the verb tells about.

X = one actor
Y = more than one actor
Z = one actor or more than one actor

	Actor(s)	Verb	Other words
1.		were watching	.
2.		wandered	.
3.		works	.
4.		will write	.
5.		found	.

Follow the outline diagram to discredit each rule.

Rules

1. All creatures with a tail have an eye.

2. All creatures with eyelashes have a pointed top.

3. All creatures with a pointed top have an eye.

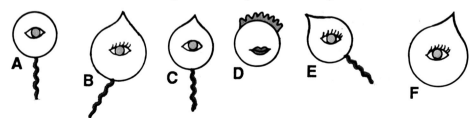

Outline diagram

To test these rules, you could examine 100 creatures.

If _____, that creature would discredit rule 1.	If _____, _____ rule 2.	If _____, _____ rule 3.

Part D | Indicate whether each verb tells about the **past, present** or **future.**

Sample Sentences		Actor(s)	Verb	Other words
	A.		walked	.
	B.		are walking	.

	Actor(s)	Verb	Other words
1.		will study	.
2.		learn	.
3.		were considering	.
4.		have	.
5.		thought	.
6.		is working	.

Part E | Follow the appropriate outline diagram to write about the problems with these arguments.

Argument 1: Janice got a call from her dad. After she came back from the call, she had tears in her eyes. Her dad must have told her some bad news.

Argument 2: Every playcr on the Tigers is an excellent player. Every player on the Tigers wears Plicco shoes. Therefore, everybody who wears Plicco shoes must be an excellent player.

Outline diagrams

```
_____          however, the conclusion _____
_____    X     _____. Evidence about _____
_____;         _____.
```

```
_____          Another possibility
_____    X     _____
_____.         _____.
```

Part F Write the letter that shows the part of speech for the last word in each sentence. If the last word is not a noun, rewrite the ending so it has one or two adjectives and a noun.

1. That city is interesting.
2. Our guide was knowledgeable.
3. The trail led to an old bridge.
4. We almost laughed about Denny's crazy conclusion.
5. Mt. McKinley is high.
6. Those alligators waited silently for carp.
7. The restaurant was profitable.
8. The news broadcast told about it.

Part G Follow the outline diagram to describe how you would test the rule.

Rule: All fires give off heat.

Outline diagram

To test the rule, you could examine _____
[how many]
_____.

If _____
_____,
the evidence would
discredit the rule.

If _____
_____,
the evidence would
not discredit the rule.

Lesson  15

Part A

For each sentence, write **X, Y** or **Z** to indicate the number of actors the verb tells about.

X = one actor

Y = more than one actor

Z = one actor or more than one actor

	Actor(s)	Verb	Other words	
1.		sold		.
2.		hear		.
3.		will read		.
4.		has purchased		.

Part B

Follow the outline diagram to write about each sentence that has a silly meaning.

1. James bought more than a radio.
2. Her friend asked more than 100 questions.
3. Linda ran farther than two miles.
4. The girls next door bought more watermelons than Michael.
5. Our doctor drives more than 80,000 miles every year.
6. Edna won more prizes than her brother.

Outline diagram

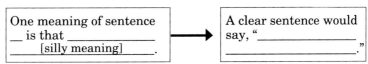

Part C Complete each rule by examining the pets shown. Then follow the outline diagram to describe the test for each rule.

Rules

1. All pets with straight hair have _____.

2. All pets with a pointed head have _____.

3. All pets with curly hair have _____.

Pets

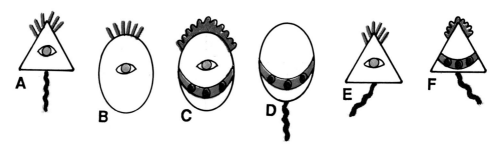

A   B   C   D   E   F

Outline diagram

To test these rules, you could _____.

| If _____, that pet would discredit rule 1. | If _____, _____ rule 2. | If _____, _____ rule 3. |

Indicate whether each verb tells about the **past, present** or **future**.

	Actor(s)	Verb	Other words
1.		looks	.
2.		were riding	.
3.		will go	.
4.		is wondering	.
5.		bought	.
6.		see	.
7.		stops	.

Independent Work

For each item, follow the appropriate outline diagram to tell about another possible interpretation.

Item 1

Mr. Graves saw Henry suddenly run from the barn, run to the well, grab a bucket of water and run back into the barn. Mr. Graves concluded that one of the animals in the barn must have been very thirsty.

Item 2

Betty left in a great hurry to go on a trip. Later, her neighbor Helen observed that the front door of Betty's house was wide open. Helen was convinced that robbers had broken into Betty's house, so Helen called the police.

Item 3

Danny loves to swim. Danny is from Texas, so all Texans must love to swim.

Lesson 16

Part A Write **X, Y** or **Z** to indicate the number of actors each verb refers to. Write **past, present** or **future.** Then write sentences that start with **he, she** or **they.**

X = one actor

Y = more than one actor

Z = one actor or more than one actor

	Actor(s)	Verb	Other words
1.		are selling	.
2.		writes	.
3.		is chasing	.
4.		bothered	.
5.		will throw	.
6.		catches	.

Table F3

Toothpaste	Soap
tube	package
soft	hard
used for cleaning teeth	used for cleaning body

- Table F3 contrasts toothpaste and soap. The table identifies three differences between toothpaste and soap.

- When you **contrast** two things, you tell about each **difference.**

- You can use two approaches. You can write parallel sentences that tell about each **difference,** or you can first tell about all the features of one thing and then tell about the parallel features of the other thing.

- Here's a passage that tells about one difference at a time:

> According to Table F3, toothpaste differs from soap in three ways. Toothpaste comes in a tube, but soap comes in a package. Toothpaste is soft, but soap is hard. Toothpaste is used to clean teeth, but soap is used to clean the body.

- Here's a passage that tells about all the features of toothpaste and then tells about the corresponding features of soap:

> According to Table F3, toothpaste differs from soap in three ways. Toothpaste comes in a tube. It is soft. And it is used to clean the teeth. Soap comes in a package. It is hard. And it is used to clean the body.

Follow the outline diagram to write about the differences.

Table F4
Facts about Male and Female
Black Widow Spiders

Male	Female
less than $\frac{1}{2}$ inch long	more than 1 inch long
not poisonous	poisonous
no red markings	red hourglass on abdomen

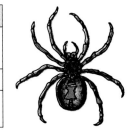

Outline diagrams

According to _____,

a male black widow spider differs from a female black widow in three ways.

1

2

3

1

2

3

1

2

3

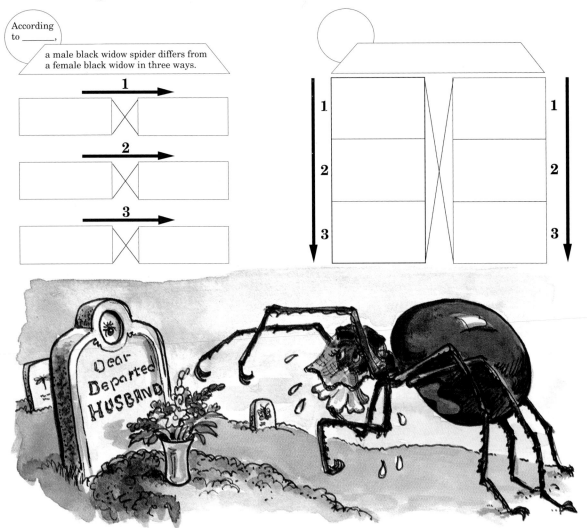

Dear Departed HUSBAND

Make up rules that describe the set of figures below.

Rules

1. All the figures with straight sides _____.

2. All the black circles _____.

3. All the black circles _____.

Figures

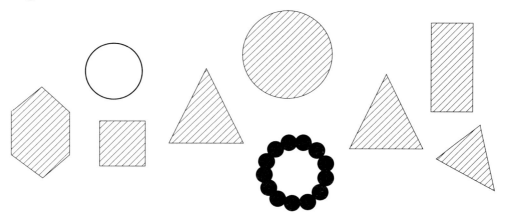

Independent Work

Part E | The arguments are not correct. Use the appropriate outline diagram to explain the problem with each argument.

Argument 1: Mary played with Linda three times last month. Mary was late on each one of those days. Therefore, Mary is late every time she plays with Linda.

Argument 2: I met two people from Dixon County. Each of them wore a straw hat. Therefore, everybody from Dixon County must wear a straw hat.

Write the letter that shows the part of speech for the last word in each sentence. If the last word is not a noun, rewrite the ending so it has one or two adjectives and a noun.

1. They hollered and waved at him.
2. The dogs became thirsty.
3. This argument confused Howard.
4. Sharon and her sisters loved watching it.
5. We took some money out of the bank.
6. The rotten log was full of them.
7. The insects made a buzzing sound.
8. The lunch was very tasty.

Part G Follow the outline diagram to write about each item.

1. Ann threw out more old possessions than her brother.
2. The dog doesn't like to eat hamburger as much as the cat.
3. My uncle said that he collected more garbage than his neighbor.

Outline diagram

| One meaning of sentence ___ is that _____ [silly meaning] _____ . | → | A clear sentence would say, " _____ _____ ." |

Lesson 17

| Follow the outline diagrams to write about the differences.

Table F5
Facts about Land
Mammals and Fish

mammals	fish
hair	scales
warm blood	cold blood
legs	fins

Outline diagrams

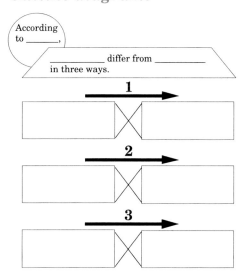

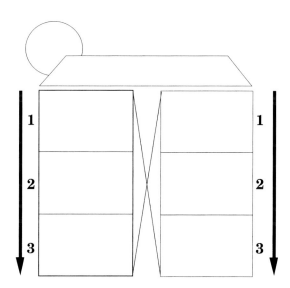

Part B | Write three rules about pets D and E.

Pets

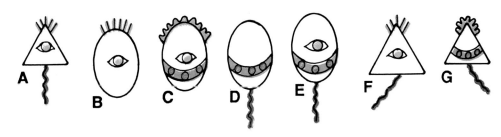

Part C | Follow the outline diagram to write a paragraph that describes which rules still hold for the pets that are bald.

A larger sample of bald pets

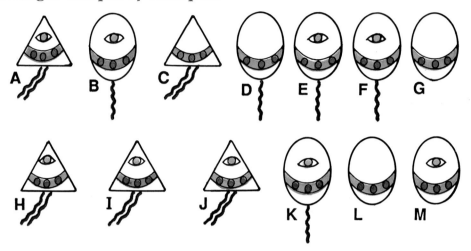

Outline diagram

The larger sample of pets discredits ___ rules.

Pets ___ discredit rule ___ because _____.

No pets discredit rule ___ because _____.

rule ___ because _____.

Part D | If the part shown for each item is a verb, write a complete sentence that uses the verb.

Sample Sentence _____ five ducks.

1. yesterday morning.
2. were swimming
3. afterwards

4. will find
5. sleeps
6. his brothers

Part E | Follow the outline diagram to write about each item.

1. John used the computer more than his teacher.

2. Amy got more information from the encyclopedia than her friends.

Outline diagram

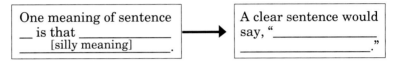

Part F | Follow the outline diagram to describe how you would test the rule.

Rule: All ocean water tastes salty.

Outline diagram

To test the rule, you could _____
                    [how much]
_____.

If _____
_____,
the evidence would
discredit the rule.

If _____
_____,
the evidence would
not discredit the rule.

Lesson 18

Part A Follow the outline diagrams to write two paragraphs that contrast Figure A and Figure B.

Figure A

3 inches

3 inches

Figure B

6 inches

5 inches

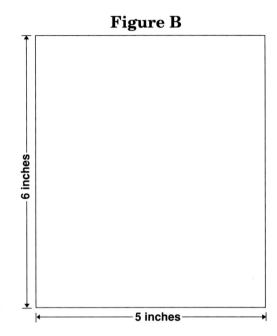

Outline diagrams

_____ differs from _____ in four ways.

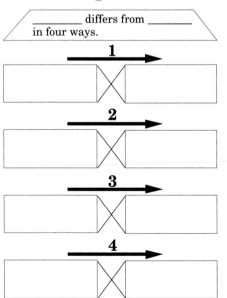

1

2

3

4

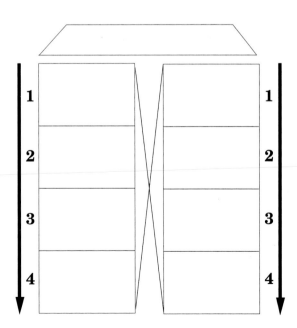

Write **X, Y** or **Z** to indicate the number of actors each verb refers to. Write **past, present** or **future.** Then write sentences that start with **he, she** or **they.**

X = one actor

Y = more than one actor

Z = one actor or more than one actor

	Actor(s)	Verb	Other words
1.		was sleeping	.
2.		has	.
3.		did	.
4.		will buy	.
5.		wanted	.
6.		was pushed	.

Write three rules about the pets with two tails.

Pets

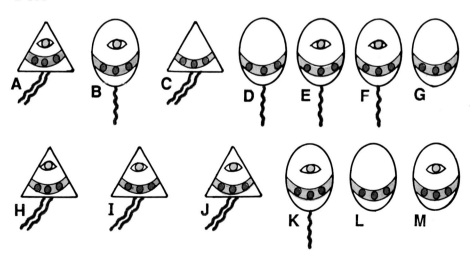

Part D

When you examine a larger sample of pets, you discover pets that discredit rules 2 and 3.

Follow the outline diagram to write about pet Z.

Outline diagram

Pet Z discredits all the rules about _____ _____ .

| Pet Z discredits rule __ because _____ . | | |

Independent Work

Part E

Use the appropriate outline diagram to write about the problem with each argument.

Argument 1: George Henderson has a whip.
A whip can be used to punish animals.
Therefore, he must use it to punish animals.

Argument 2: Marie does exercises every day.
Push-ups are exercises.
Therefore, she must do push-ups every day.

Write the conclusion of each argument.

Argument 1:   All arguments have a conclusion.
              Mary made up an argument.

 .

Argument 2:   All row crops grow in Green Valley.
              Corn is a row crop.

 .

Argument 3:   On hotter days, water evaporates faster.
              The seventh of July was one of the hotter days.

 .

Argument 4:   All types of rare stones were in the collection.
              Diamonds are rare stones.

 .

Argument 5:   Bill loves all types of pasta.
              Fettucine is a type of pasta.

 .

Write two or three words to replace the last word in each sentence. Label your words as adjectives and nouns.

1. The fire was bright.
2. Lucy ran down the stairs and tripped on it.
3. My uncle is skinny.
4. The hounds howled as they followed it.
5. They insisted on rewriting it.

Lesson

For each item, write the verb; then indicate whether it refers to **past, present** or **future.**

1. They were sitting near the stream.
2. Andy is in a bad mood today.
3. Jenny lost her wallet.
4. Our class will complete a large project.
5. The program is making me very tired.
6. My uncle will drive us to the beach.
7. Those animals are running from flies.
8. We spent two hours on that passage.
9. The campers are walking home.
10. Seven dogs sniffed the trail.

Write two paragraphs that contrast Figure A and Figure B.

Figure A

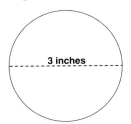

Figure B

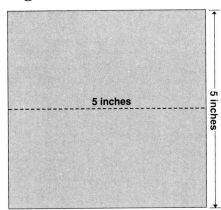

Outline diagrams

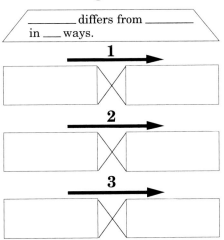

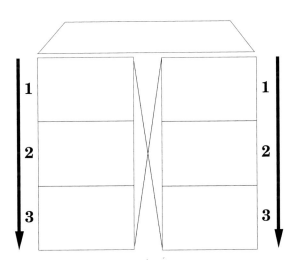

Part C | Write three words that will replace the last word in each sentence. Write the letter for the part of speech for each word in the new ending.

1. Three wolves followed them.

2. The constant motion of the waves weakened them.

3. Her observations discredited it.

4. The newspaper had an article about it.

Follow the outline diagram to write two paragraphs that discredit Mrs. Johnson's rules.

Pets

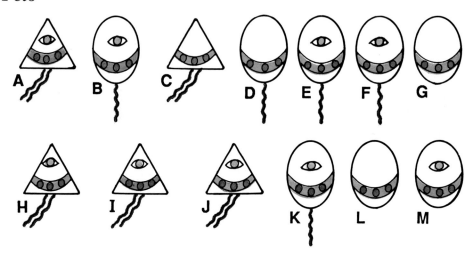

Mrs. Johnson's rules

1. All pets without tails have a round head.

2. All pets without tails have a collar.

3. All pets without tails are bald.

Outline diagram

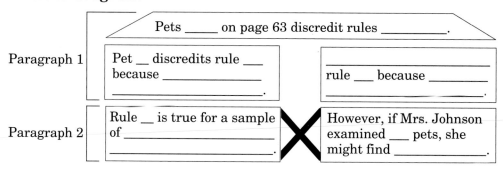

Part E | Follow the outline diagram to describe how you would test the rule.

Rule: Water boils at a lower temperature when it's at the top of a high mountain.

Outline diagram

> To test the rule, you could _____
> _____ .

> If _____
> _____ ,
> the evidence would
> discredit the rule.

> If _____
> _____ ,
> the evidence would
> not discredit the rule.

Part F | Rewrite each sentence that has a silly meaning.

1. The rabbit ate more than three mice.
2. The rabbit ate more than 36 grams of fat.
3. Bees like nectar as much as flies.
4. John loved the new truck much more than his wife.
5. Ellen purchased more than her friend Janice.

Lesson 20 – Test 2

Part A For each item, write **X, Y** or **Z** to indicate the number of actors the verb refers to. Write **past, present** or **future.** Then write sentences that start with **he, she** or **they.**

X = one actor
Y = more than one actor
Z = one actor or more than one actor

	Actor(s)	**Verb**	**Other words**
1.		were listening	.
2.		wants	.
3.		will bother	.
4.		wrote	.

Part B Follow the outline diagram to describe how you would test the rule.

Rule: All things that are made of wood float in water.

Outline diagram

> To test the rule, you could _____ _____
> _____ .
>   [how many]

> If _____
> _____ ,
> the evidence would
> discredit the rule.

> If _____
> _____ ,
> the evidence would
> not discredit the rule.

Follow the outline diagram to write two paragraphs that contrast dog A and dog B.

Dog A

Outline diagrams

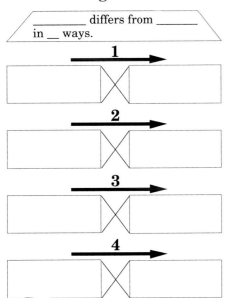

_____ differs from _____
in __ ways.

1

2

3

4

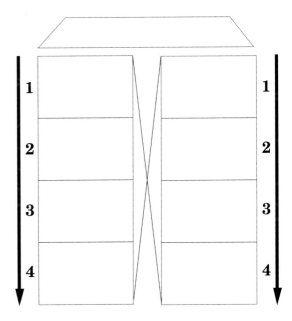

Lesson 21

Part A

- For some purposes, your writing should be very specific. How specific you are when you write depends on how specific you must be to avoid confusion.

- If you describe a lost cat as a gray-and-black striped cat, you are probably not being specific enough because there are a lot of gray-and-black striped cats. Some are big and some are little. Some are male and some are female. Some were last seen in one part of town and some were last seen in other parts.

- The more specific you are, the more confusion you can avoid.

Part B Complete the sentence so that anybody reading the description would identify the correct paper.

Statement: Andy used lined paper.

Andy used lined paper that _____

_____.

A   B   C   D

Rewrite each sentence that has a silly meaning.

1. They recycled more than old bottles.
2. Amy painted more than Milton.
3. Their house is older than our house.
4. We collected more than the people on the beach.
5. Sasha ran faster than Margaret ran.
6. The cupboard contained more than cups.
7. The contest lasted longer than four hours.

Outline diagram

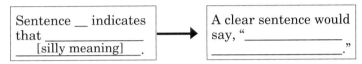

Sentence ___ indicates that _____ ___[silly meaning]___ .

A clear sentence would say, "_____ _____."

Part D For each sentence, write the verb words and **past, present** or **future** to tell about each sentence.

1. Henry is traveling with his parents.
2. Helen ran with the other runners.
3. The zebra was staring at the leopard for a long time.
4. The longest line was near the cash register.
5. His argument had many poor sentences.
6. Our teacher will help him figure out the answer.
7. The girls laughed whenever Morris acted silly.
8. A large cloud is moving in front of the sun.
9. Our cousins will come to the picnic.
10. The mice are sneaking around the corners.

Use the outline diagram to write two paragraphs responding to Roger's statement.

Table F8

Ranking of fastest race cars	Number of races won in 20 races	Number of mechanical failures in 20 races
1. Fenos	0	17
2. Bumpos	2	0
3. Lemps	14	3

Roger Pike's statement

Fenos are the best race cars because they are the fastest cars.

Outline diagram

_____ Pike concludes that _____
_____.

The evidence for his conclusion is that _____ _____ ;

however, the evidence is inadequate.

If Fenos were _____ _____ , Table F8 would indicate _____ . _____ also _____ _____ .

However, the table indicates that _____ __ _____ and _____ _____ .

Part F Write letters to indicate the part of speech for the last word in each sentence.

1. The dog followed a strong scent.

2. The hunters followed him.

3. The early morning air was still.

4. They questioned her meaning.

5. Our dog loves to play in the water.

6. She shakes when she is wet.

7. How long did it take to fix all of them?

8. She helped me.

9. They started to get excited.

10. Could that adventure lead to a disaster?

Part G Use the chart and the outline diagram to write about the differences between spring and fall.

Chart

Facts about spring	Facts about fall
days get longer	days get shorter
ends just before longest day of year	ends just before shortest day of year
growth of plants speeds up	growth of plants slows down

Outline diagram

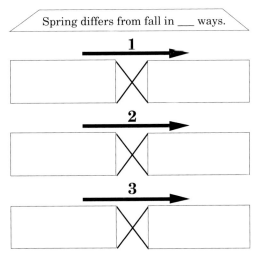

Spring differs from fall in ___ ways.

1

2

3

Lesson 22

Part A   Use the outline diagram to write two paragraphs responding to Judy's statement.

Table F8

Ranking of fastest race cars	Number of races won in 20 races	Number of mechanical failures in 20 races
1. Fenos	0	17
2. Bumpos	2	0
3. Lemps	14	3

Judy Pike's statement

Lemps are the worst race cars because they are the slowest race cars.

Outline diagram

_____ Pike concludes that _____
_____.

| The evidence for her conclusion is that _____ _____; | however, the evidence is inadequate. |
| If Lemps were _____ _____, Table F8 would indicate _____. _____ also _____ _____. | However, the table indicates that _____ _____ and _____ _____. |

Describe the differences in these papers.

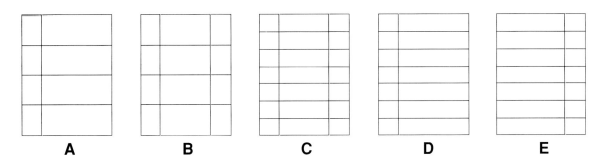

A   B   C   D   E

Write a question about each difference in the group of papers.

Differences

1. the spacing of the lines

2. the number of margins

3. the side on which the margin appears

Does the paper have _____ ?

Part D

- You've written about the strange pets. You've worked with rules that were supposed to be true of all members of the group. If a rule told about bald pets, the rule was supposed to be true for every bald pet. You discredited rules by finding **just one pet** that did not follow the rule.

- Some rules are different because they can't be discredited by finding one individual that breaks the rule.

- Here's an example:

  Men are stronger than women.

- If we found a woman who was stronger than 500 men, we would not discredit the rule.

- Here's another example:

  The Tiger football team is the tallest team in the city.

- We could find a player from another team that is taller than the tallest Tiger, but the evidence would not discredit the rule about the Tigers. The Tigers are the tallest team if the total height of that team is more than the total height of any other team in the city.

- Here's the rule about **groups:**

  If the statement tells about the **whole group** and not every individual in the group, evidence about one individual will not discredit the statement.

Part E

1. Every player on the Tigers is over six feet tall.

2. The Tigers eat over 60 pounds of vegetables every day.

3. The official uniform of the Tigers is red and gold.

Two of the statements can be discredited by referring to individuals. For each of those statements, follow the outline diagram, describe your test and tell what the outcomes would mean.

1. The Tigers decided to play three night games.

2. The Tigers had a record of 19 wins and only 1 loss.

3. The Tigers prefer Bumpo automobiles.

4. The tallest player on the Tigers is 6 feet 7 inches tall.

5. The Tigers are the fastest team in the league.

6. Every player on the Tigers eats at least 2 pounds of vegetables every day of the week.

Outline diagram

To test statement __, you could
_____.

If _____
_____,
the evidence would
discredit statement __.

If _____
_____,
the evidence would not
discredit statement __.

Part G | Use the chart and the outline diagram to write about the differences between traveling by plane and by ship.

Chart **Trip from San Francisco, California, to Fairbanks, Alaska**

Facts if traveling by plane	Facts if traveling by ship
takes 5 hours	takes 12 days
passengers don't move around much	passengers move around more
can land 1 mile from city	can dock 250 miles from city

Outline diagram

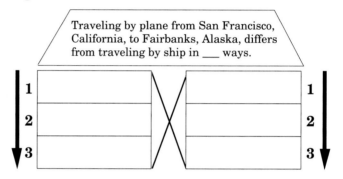

Traveling by plane from San Francisco, California, to Fairbanks, Alaska, differs from traveling by ship in ___ ways.

1 2 3   1 2 3

Part H | Follow the outline diagram to write a paragraph about which race car is actually the best. Refer to the evidence in Table F8.

Table F8

Ranking of fastest race cars	Number of races won in 20 races	Number of mechanical failures in 20 races
1. Fenos	0	17
2. Bumpos	2	0
3. Lemps	14	3

Outline diagram

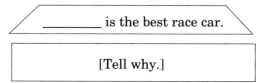

_____ is the best race car.

[Tell why.]

Lesson 23

Part A — Follow the outline diagram to write about Dale's statement.

Table F8

Ranking of fastest race cars	Number of races won in 20 races	Number of mechanical failures in 20 races
1. Fenos	0	17
2. Bumpos	2	0
3. Lemps	14	3

Dale Pike's statement

Bumpos are the best race cars because they had no mechanical failures in 20 races.

Outline diagram

_____ Pike concludes that _____
_____.

The evidence for his conclusion is that _____ _____;

however, the evidence is inadequate.

If Bumpos were _____ _____, Table F8 would indicate _____.

However, the table indicates that _____.

- For some situations, you don't need sentences that are very specific. For other situations, you must be more specific. How specific your sentences should be depends on the possibilities.

- Here is a sentence:

The girl touched the triangle.

- The sentence is specific enough for one of the pictures below, but not specific enough for the other picture.

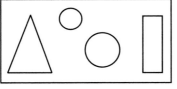

Picture A

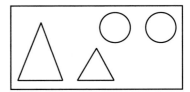

Picture B

Part C For each item, write the letter of the picture the sentence tells about. Then rewrite each item so it tells about the picture with more than one like object.

Item 1: She touched the striped circle.

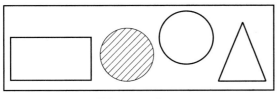

Picture A

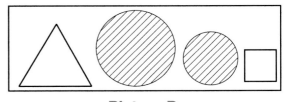

Picture B

Item 2: She touched the square.

Picture A

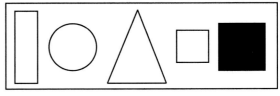

Picture B

Item 3: She touched a spotted rectangle.

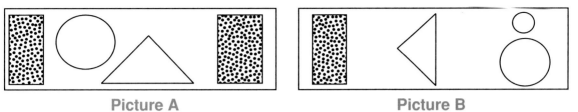

Picture A   Picture B

Item 4: She touched a curved line.

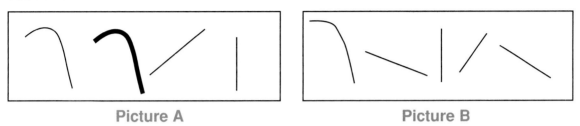

Picture A   Picture B

Item 5: She touched a circle that is on a triangle.

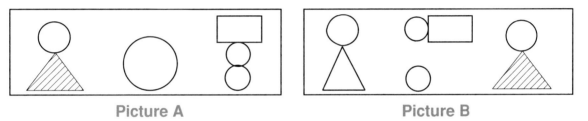

Picture A   Picture B

For each item, write the verb; indicate whether it refers to **past**, **present** or **future**.

1. The girls are discussing the problem.
2. Bonnie's argument has many flaws.
3. Those butterflies had strange habits.
4. That car is becoming very rusty.
5. Her aunt was going to dinner.
6. The chairs were heavy.
7. She talks very fast.
8. The farmer pointed south.
9. Five kittens were tussling in the grass.
10. The story will end within five minutes.

Write the number of each statement that can be discredited by information about one individual.

1. Redwoods are very tall trees.
2. The Tigers played 11 games last year.
3. The oldest living tree is in southern California.
4. There is not one single potato bug in Green Valley.
5. All wood that is thoroughly dried will float in water.
6. Roundo tires last longer than any other tires.
7. The residents of Fromo, Nebraska, have a very high annual income.

Part F | Write about the problem with each argument. Use the appropriate outline diagram.

Argument 1: Milly's dog has a black tongue. Her dog is mean. Therefore, all dogs with a black tongue are mean.

Argument 2: Henry got injured while playing on a playground. Therefore, playing on a playground is dangerous for all children.

Part G | Follow the outline diagram to discredit the rule.

Rule: All things made of brass are attracted to a magnet.

Outline diagram

To test the rule, you could _____ _____.

Lesson 24

- Some sentences tell about things that are always true. The verbs in these sentences tell about the **present**.

- Here are some sentences:

  Airplanes fly.

  Bulls weigh **more than rabbits.**

  Gravity pulls **objects toward the center of the earth.**

- Here's a situation:

  For five years, Terry has liked strawberries. He likes them now, and he'll probably like them tomorrow.

- Here's how we express that idea:

  Terry likes **strawberries.**

- Here's another situation:

  Although some birds do not fly, most of them are capable of flying. They may not be flying at this moment, but if they need to, they can fly.

- Here's how we express that idea:

  Most birds fly.

- The verb refers to present time even though some of the birds that can fly are not flying.

- Here's another situation:

  Although it is possible for strange weather patterns to occur, if a person went higher and higher in the atmosphere, the air would get thinner and thinner. That means there would be less air the higher the person went.

- Here's how we could express that idea:

  As you go **higher in the atmosphere, the air** gets **thinner.**

For each item, write a sentence with a verb that refers to present time.

1. Dorothy examined eagles and noticed that all of them were covered with feathers. She examined robins, sparrows and hawks. She even examined penguins. She concluded that all of them had feathers. She then wrote a sentence that told about all birds.

2. Dorothy also discovered that the robins she observed made sounds. The sparrows, the hawks and the penguins also made sounds.

3. On more than four occasions, meteorologists observed that hailstones fell from cumulonimbus clouds. On no occasion did the meteorologists observe hailstones falling from other types of clouds.

4. Gregory noted that 14 dogs wagged their tail when they seemed to be happy. Three of those dogs had stubby little tails. Gregory made up a sentence about dogs and their tails.

Part C

- You've discredited statements that tell about individuals. You found just one individual who broke the rule.

- You do the same thing when you discredit statements about groups, but you must use information **about the group,** not about individuals that make up the group.

The Tigers played 11 games last year.

Item 1: Before the season began, the Tigers were scheduled to play 12 games.

Item 2: According to Reverend Dundee, the Tigers played 14 games.

Item 3: Four of the players on the Tigers missed six games.

Item 4: There was a terrible snowstorm on one day that the Tigers were scheduled to play, and they did not play on that day.

Item 5: The original schedule had 12 games, but 2 games were canceled.

Part E | Write the number of each item that discredits the statement.

Last year, the Tigers ate more types of vegetables than the Bolts ate.

Item 1: The Bolts ate 600 pounds of carrots, but the Tigers ate only 365 pounds of carrots.

Item 2: The Bolts ate four more types of vegetables than the Tigers ate.

Item 3: The Bolts ate more than 56 different types of vegetables.

Item 4: The Bolts ate 91 types of vegetables, but the Tigers ate only 87 types of vegetables.

Item 5: Three members of the Bolts are vegetarians.

Item 6: The Bolts ate seven types of vegetables that the Tigers did not eat.

For each item, write the letter of the picture that could be described with a less specific sentence. Then rewrite your sentence so it tells only about that picture.

Item 1: She touched the striped triangle.

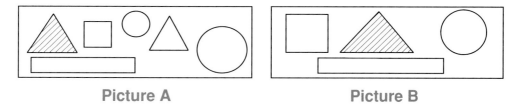

Picture A   Picture B

Item 2: She touched the large striped square.

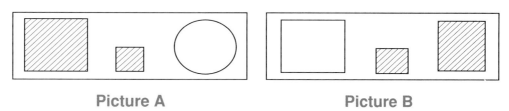

Picture A   Picture B

Item 3: She touched the circle on top of the black triangle.

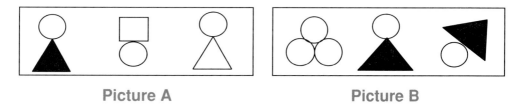

Picture A   Picture B

Item 4: She touched the straight line.

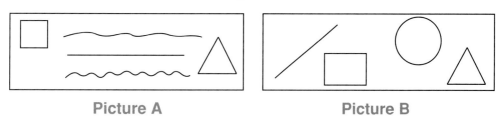

Picture A   Picture B

Table F9 – Leading Running Shoes

Shoes	Quality	Ranked by 600 runners	Price
Rompo	poor	59th	$21.00
Fleetfoot	excellent	2nd	$36.00
Skidmore	good	3rd	$58.00

Roger Pike's statement

Rompos are the best buy because they cost less than any other leading shoe.

Outline diagram

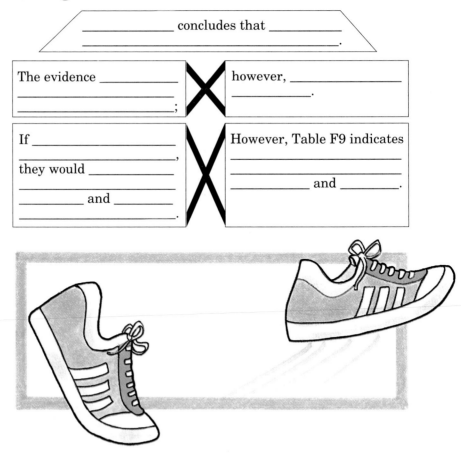

_____ concludes that _____
_____.

The evidence _____
_____
_____;

however, _____
_____.

If _____
_____,
they would _____
_____
_____ and _____
_____.

However, Table F9 indicates
_____
_____
_____ and _____.

Part H | Write about the shoe you think is best.

Table F9 – Leading Running Shoes

Shoes	Quality	Ranked by 600 runners	Price
Rompo	poor	59th	$21.00
Fleetfoot	excellent	2nd	$36.00
Skidmore	good	3rd	$58.00

Outline diagram

_____ is the best buy.

[Tell why.]

Part I | Rewrite each sentence by replacing the last word with a noun and at least one adjective. Indicate the part of speech of each word in your new ending.

1. They looked beyond it.

2. Our class observed them.

3. My report describes it.

Lesson 25

Part A

Each sentence works for two of the three pictures. Write the letters for those pictures. Rewrite the sentence so it is less specific and tells about only **one** of the pictures. Then rewrite the sentence so it is specific enough to tell about the third picture.

Item 1: He touched the striped circle.

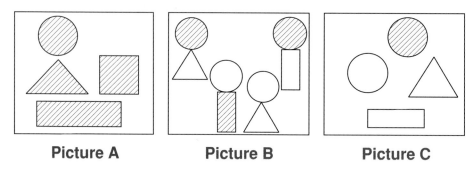

Picture A   **Picture B**   **Picture C**

Item 2: He touched the black triangle.

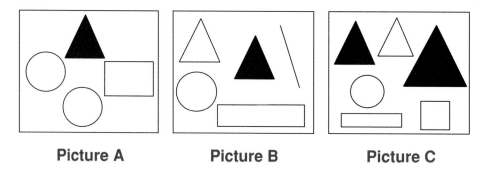

Picture A   **Picture B**   **Picture C**

Part B

- You're going to do a lot of work with **consistency** and **inconsistency.**

- When two things are **inconsistent,** they do not agree with each other. In some situations, things are not consistent with what you would expect. These things are not necessarily wrong; they are just things you would not expect.

- Remember, **consistent** means that things agree with each other. **Inconsistent** means they don't agree.

Part C | For each item, write the letter of the choice that is most consistent with the facts given.

Item 1. *Facts:* Mr. Taylor is 80 years old. He has 7 married children. The oldest is 52. The youngest is 34.

A. Mr. Taylor has no grandchildren.

B. Mr. Taylor has many grandchildren.

C. Mr. Taylor has one grandchild.

Item 2. *Facts:* It is now June. There was a great deal of rain this spring. The rain continued throughout the month of May.

A. There is practically no danger of forest fires.

B. There is a great danger of forest fires.

C. The forest fires occurred in April, and there are no forests left in the area.

Item 3. *Facts:* Mrs. Anderson loves plants. For 26 years, she worked in a florist shop. She has a large home with an enormous backyard.

A. She has a tiny garden.

B. She has no garden at all.

C. She has a large, beautiful garden.

Item 4. Write facts for Mrs. Jones. Make the facts consistent with choice A in Item 3.

Part D

- You can combine some sentences by using the word **who** or **that.**
- You use the word **who** to refer to humans. You use the word **that** to refer to things that are not human.

For each item, write **A** or **B** for the correct sentence part.

Item 1: A. cars **that** are on the highways
B. cars **who** are on the highways

Item 2: A. a man **who** was happy
B. a man **that** was happy

Item 3: A. girls **that** do well in school
B. girls **who** do well in school

Item 4: A. trees **who** have broken branches
B. trees **that** have broken branches

Part F

- You can combine sentences by using the words **who** or **that.**
- Here are sample sentences that can be combined:

    They had **bikes.**
    The **bikes** were new.

- Here's the combined sentence:

    They had **bikes** **that** were new.

- Here's another pair of sentences that can be combined:

    The **students** made a poster.
    Those **students** studied art.

- Here's the combined sentence:

    The **students** **who** studied art made a poster.

- Here are the steps:
    ✔ Find the part of the first sentence that is **repeated.**
    ✔ Change the second sentence so it starts with **who** or **that.**
    ✔ Write all the words from the first sentence.
    ✔ Put the changed second sentence **just after the repeated part.**

For each item, write the combined sentence.

1. Boys entered the race.
   Those boys were in good condition.

2. Jim watched the boat.
   The boat was going under the bridge.

3. The notebook was almost empty.
   The notebook slipped from her desk.

4. The people purchased hot dogs and popcorn.
   The people were at the ball park.

- Some statements seem to tell about groups; however, they actually tell about **every** individual in the group.

- Here is a statement of that type:

  ### Mammals are warm blooded.

- That's a rule about every mammal. You could discredit that rule if you found one healthy mammal that was not warm blooded.

- The easiest way to figure out whether the statement tells about all individuals in the group or about the entire group is to ask whether information about one individual could be used to discredit the statement.

Write yes or no to tell whether each statement can be discredited by information about one individual.

1. Dogs are larger than house cats.

2. Healthy insects have six legs.

3. Rabbits were in the front yard.

4. Dogs are full grown when they are one year old.

5. All healthy bears have fur.

6. Bears love to catch fish.

For each item, write the verb; indicate whether it refers to **past, present** or **future.**

1. All birds have beaks.

2. This spring, more than 500 alligators will hatch on Gator Island.

3. Their alligator chased his baby rabbit.

4. Gwen looks very attractive today.

5. The train will be at the station soon.

6. The rabbits were playing with the alligator.

7. I saw only four rabbits.

8. We started with 11 rabbits.

9. Alligators are first cousins of crocodiles.

Part K | Follow the outline diagram to tell what is wrong with Arnold's decision.

Arnold's decision

Arnold selected the Gold Club Ranch as the vacation spot for the Jackson family. However, his choice does not meet all the Jackson family's requirements.

Jackson family's requirements

1. The Jackson family does not want to travel more than 600 miles.
2. The vacation spot cannot cost more than $100 per day.
3. The vacation spot must offer horseback riding, swimming and tennis.

Facts

Resorts	Distance from home	Activities	Cost per day
Hi Ho Mountain	832 miles	horseback riding, tennis, swimming, volleyball, horseshoes	$89
Laid Back Ranch	438 miles	volleyball, horseback riding, hiking, horseshoes, fishing	$99
Rest More Ranch	486 miles	horseback riding, horseshoes, volleyball, tennis, swimming, golf	$96
Gold Club Ranch	446 miles	horseback riding, tennis, swimming, boating, fishing, hiking, camping	$107

Outline diagram

The vacation spot that Arnold selected does not meet all the Jackson family's requirements.

The Jackson family wants _____ _____; ✕ however, the Gold Club Ranch _____ _____.

Arnold should have selected _____. = [Tell why.]

Lesson 26

Part A | For each item, use **who** or **that** to write the combined sentence.

1. They found a small box. The small box contained old coins.
2. A car stopped suddenly. The car had a dented door.
3. Tim noticed an old man. The old man walked with a limp.
4. The woman lives in California. The woman bought our house.
5. We slipped on the ice. The ice covered our front sidewalk.

Part B | Accounts should be consistent about time, but some accounts are not consistent. Those accounts describe what happened in the **past** but may have some sentences that refer to the present.

Rewrite each sentence that refers to the present so that it refers to the past.

Passage

Linda and Andrew almost had a serious accident. They were crossing a small stream. A support on the bridge broke. Suddenly, the bridge tilts to one side. Andrew almost falls off. He grabs Linda. Then she almost slid off the bridge with him. Finally, Andrew grabbed a rail. He hung onto it, and Linda climbed over him. She got off the bridge first.

In the meantime, Andrew is losing his grip on the rail. A young man came by and saw what happened. He crawled out to where Andrew was and helped Andrew get off the bridge.

- You've worked with statements about all individuals in a group and statements about groups themselves.

- Some arguments draw faulty conclusions because the arguments confuse groups with individuals.

- Here are rules:
    1. Evidence about **an individual** within a group does not lead to a proper conclusion about **the group.**
    2. Evidence about **one individual** does not lead to a proper conclusion about **another individual.**
    3. Evidence about **a group** does not lead to a proper conclusion about **an individual** within the group.

- Here's a faulty argument:

    John is very rude. John is a member of the Tigers. Therefore, everybody on the Tigers must be very rude.

- You've worked with this type of argument before. The conclusion is more general than the evidence. The evidence about the individual does not lead to a proper conclusion about the Tigers.

- Here's another faulty argument:

    Tim is a member of the Tigers, and Tim is an excellent player. Herb is also a member of the Tigers. So Herb must be an excellent player.

- That conclusion about Herb is not proper because it is based on evidence about an individual. Evidence about one individual within a group cannot lead to a proper conclusion about another individual.

- Here's another faulty argument:

    The Tigers are the best team in the city. George is a member of the Tigers. Therefore, George must be one of the best players in the city.

- The conclusion about George is not proper. It is based on evidence about **the group.** Evidence about the group cannot lead to a proper conclusion about the individuals within the group.

Part D

Use the rules in part C and follow the outline diagram below to write about each argument.

> **Argument 1:** Mrs. Anderson's class is very good in math. Diane is in Mrs. Anderson's class. Therefore, Diane must be very good in math.
>
> **Argument 2:** Jean Epstein is very athletic. She has a sister, Charlene. Charlene must also be very athletic.
>
> **Argument 3:** Mrs. Hansen owns a Bumpo, and it's a very reliable car. Edna Franklin also owns a Bumpo. She must find it very reliable.

Outline diagram

Argument __ uses evidence about _____ to draw a conclusion about _____.	However, evidence about _____ does not lead to a proper conclusion about _____.

For each item, the sentence is not specific enough for one of the pictures. Write the letter for that picture. Then rewrite the sentence so it's specific enough to tell about the first object in that picture.

Item 1:   She saw the man.

Item 2:   She saw the car.

Item 3:   She saw a tree.

Part F | For each argument, follow the outline diagram.

Argument 1: Vegetables are needed for a balanced diet.
Kenya eats a well-balanced diet.
Therefore, she eats a lot of carrots.

Argument 2: The Thompsons indicate that they are very
pleased with their new car.
Bumpos have many satisfied customers.
Therefore, the Thompsons must have bought
a Bumpo.

Outline diagram

Part G | Copy each sentence. Write the letter to show the part of speech for each underlined word.

1. Tom felt sad.

2. Our dog barked last night.

3. That man ordered a large pizza.

4. We studied the sun.

5. Their argument was clear.

6. The TV program was dull.

Lesson 27

Part A Rewrite each sentence so it has a part that begins with **who** or **that** and tells about the first object in the picture.

Sample: He met a woman.

Item 1: He saw a car.

Item 2: He met a boy.

Item 3: She followed the woman.

Follow the outline diagram to write about each argument.

Argument 1: Nan has a police dog. It is the friendliest and nicest dog I've ever seen. Therefore, all police dogs must be friendly and well behaved.

Argument 2: The Tigers eat more vegetables than the Bolts eat. Greg is a Bolt. Therefore, he must eat fewer vegetables than any Tiger eats.

Argument 3: Karla's Bumpo is very reliable. That means all Bumpos are reliable.

Outline diagram

Argument __ uses evidence about _____ to draw a conclusion about _____ .

However, evidence about _____ does not lead to a proper conclusion about _____ .

Part C

- Here's a rule about rewriting sentences so they refer to the past:

  ✔ If the sentence uses the word **will,** you often change it so it has the word **would.**

  ✔ If the sentence uses the word **can,** you often change it so it has the word **could.**

- Here's a sentence that uses the word **will:**

  Bob **indicates** that he **will** finish his work by 3 p.m.

- Here's the sentence rewritten so it refers to the past:

  Bob **indicated** that he **would** finish his work by 3 p.m.

- Here's a sentence that uses the word **can:**

  Jenny **tells** me that she **can** pick up Friday's mail.

- Here's the sentence rewritten so it refers to the past:

  Jenny **told** me that she **could** pick up Friday's mail.

Part D   Rewrite each sentence so it refers to the past. Use the word **would** or **could.**

1. Mr. Green indicates that he can give us a hand.
2. The girls say that they will put out the campfire soon.
3. Gwen says that she can hear mice in the walls.
4. George insists that he will not work on Saturday.
5. Leah tells me that I can take the A train.

Part E   Make up house prices that are consistent with the information given in the pictures.

① _____   ② __ $70,000 __

③ _____   ④ _____

Part F — Copy each sentence. Write the letter to show the part of speech for each underlined word.

1. That cat catches butterflies.

2. They watched us.

3. The argument was faulty.

4. Our car had broken windows.

5. The students completed them.

6. The Panthers played a great game.

Part G — Rewrite each sentence that has a silly meaning.

1. The bulldozer tore down more than the tractor.

2. Quincy built more than his brother.

3. My sister loves cookies more than cake.

4. She liked the book more than Darlene.

Lesson 28

Part A | Follow the outline diagram to write about each argument that is not sound.

Argument 1: The team that won the most games is the champion. The Stars won more games than any other team. Therefore, the Stars are the champions.

Argument 2: The cost of dinner was more than the cost of lunch. The cost of dinner was $6.50. Therefore, the cost of lunch was less than $6.50.

Argument 3: The Tigers practice five days a week. Cindy is a Tiger. Therefore, she must have been at practice five days last week.

Argument 4: Tim drives a yellow car. Tim is very lazy. Wendy also drives a yellow car. It must be true that she's lazy.

Argument 5: All the Jets can do at least 50 push-ups. Mitch is a Jet. Therefore, Mitch must be able to do at least 50 push-ups.

Outline diagram

| Argument __ uses evidence about _____ to _____ _____. | However, evidence about _____ does not lead _____. |

- Some words in a sentence may look like verbs, but they are not verbs.

- Words are not verbs in a sentence unless they tell about the past, the present or the future.

- Here are different sentences with the words **to go:**

   They will decide to go to the store.
   They decide to go to the store.
   They decided to go to the store.

- The words **to go** appear in all these sentences.

- Those words do not tell about the past, the present or the future. So they are not verbs in the sentences.

- Remember, only the verb words in the sentence tell about the time.

For each sentence, write the verb. Then write **past, present** or **future** to tell about the time period.

1. Driving in the snow was very difficult for Edna.

2. All those things are not in good working condition.

3. My uncle will help us to build the bird house.

4. Her silly argument makes me want to scream.

5. Running early in the morning is a nice experience.

6. The beans are ready to be picked.

7. Your sister can help us in fixing my bike.

Copy and fill in the table. Make it consistent with the facts given about the doctors.

Table F10

Doctor	Annual earnings	Type of house	Vehicles that doctor owns	Type of neighborhood
Dr. Marks	$125,000	large, expensive	2 cars, a boat	very nice
Dr. Ukimo	$35,000			
Dr. Jones				
Dr. Johnson				

Fact 1: Dr. Marks is a pretty good eye doctor.

Fact 2: Dr. Jones is the most brilliant eye specialist in the state.

Fact 3: Dr. Johnson is just starting a practice. He finished school last spring.

Fact 4: Dr. Ukimo works with poor communities in Africa. She gives many free eye examinations.

Independent Work

Part E | Write about the problem with this argument.

Argument: Angela told me that the weather was bad on her vacation. It must have snowed a lot.

A. Rewrite each sentence so it is specific enough to tell about the first object. Use the word **who** or **that.**
B. Rewrite each sentence so it is general enough to tell about all the objects.

Item 1:   I talked to the man.

Item 2:   He stood at the bus stop.

Part A

- You've learned to combine sentences.

- Here are two sentences:

    Our neighbors have a new car.

    Those neighbors live across the street.

- In some situations, you would not need the second sentence to describe the neighbors.

- Here's that kind of situation:

Map A

N = neighbor
U = us

The only neighbors we have live across the street.

- So we do not need the more specific sentence to tell which neighbors we are referring to.

- Here's a different situation:

Map B

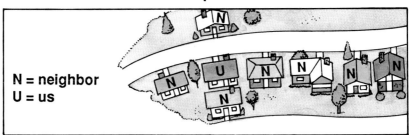

N = neighbor
U = us

We have lots of neighbors.

- So we need the more specific sentence to describe the neighbors we're referring to. If it just said, "Our neighbors," we wouldn't know which ones have the new car.

    Our neighbors who live across the street have a new car.

Part B For one of the pictures, write the combined sentence. For the other picture, write just the **first sentence.**

Item 1: Jeremy's cat was in the grass. The grass was very long.

Item 2: The car was a stolen vehicle. The car was parked at the corner.

Item 3: The girls bought a book. The book tells about animals in Africa.

Rewrite each item so it tells about the past.

1. Sam tells me that Emily will go to France on her vacation. Sam says that her brother plans to go with her.

2. Working on the farm makes Rachel very strong. She likes to do some farm work. Her mother says that Rachel does not like to clean out the barn.

Copy and fill in the table, making it consistent with the fact and the information already given in the table.

Fact: All vacation packages are offered by the same airline. The airfare is based on the number of miles.

Table F11 – Vacation Trips

Location	Distance	Airfare	Rooms	Hotel grounds and view	Total cost for 4 people, 3 days (including airfare)
Point Vista	450 miles	$450	very large	excellent	$1000
Point Terra		$900			$1500
Point Hope	200 miles		tiny	okay	
Point Away		$800			$3000

Part E | Write about the problems with each argument. Use the appropriate outline diagram.

Argument 1: Eddie Nelson is one of the best workers I have ever seen. I'll bet the entire Nelson family is a hardworking family.

Argument 2: I went to Vern's Restaurant and had a chicken sandwich that was not very good. I'll bet Vern's pizza is as bad as the chicken sandwich.

Argument 3: Brandon High has the worst football team in the city. Denny plays on that team. He must be a terrible player.

Lesson 30 – Test 3

Part A Rewrite each sentence so it tells about the past.

1. Rita indicates that Mary will miss school next week.

2. Diana tells Bob that she can go with us.

Part B Some sentences in the following paragraph tell about the present. Rewrite those sentences so they tell about the past.

    A car stalled on the train tracks. Suddenly, the train comes around the bend. It is blowing its whistle. When it was only 100 yards from the car, the car started. The car moves off the track just in time.

Part C Follow the outline diagram to write about the problem in each argument.

Argument 1: Tommy has a lot of accidents. That means that Tommy's sister must have a lot of accidents, too.

Argument 2: Mr. Baxter comes from California. He's very wealthy. Therefore, everybody who comes from California must be wealthy.

Outline diagram

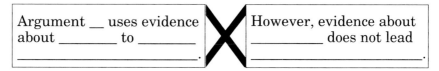

For one of the pictures, write the combined sentence. For the other picture, write just the first sentence.

Item 1: Jan's cat sat on the windowsill. The windowsill was dry.

 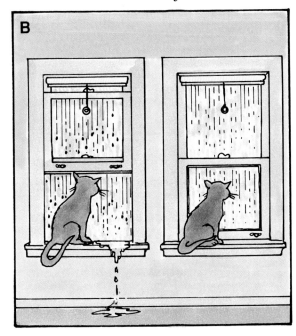

Item 2: The woman owned four cars. The woman sat next to Henry.

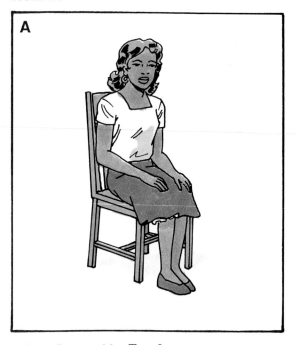 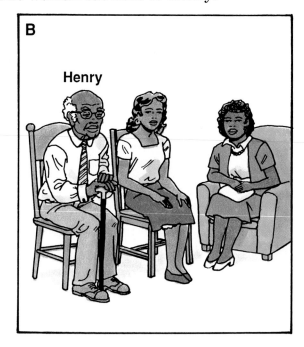

Part A | Rewrite each sentence so it tells about the past.

My mother wants to remodel the kitchen. She feels that she does not have enough counter space. My dad keeps telling her that we do not have enough money to make all the changes she wants. She points out that it will not cost too much if my sister and I do most of the work.

Part B | For one of the pictures, write the **combined sentence.** For the other picture, write just the **first sentence.**

Item 1: The woman has three children. The woman is wearing a white jacket.

Item 2: They bought the house. The house had three chimneys.

Part C

- Some words are **adverbs.** Adverbs tell **where** or **when** or **how.**
- Here are sentences that end with adverbs:

  They went **north. North** tells **where.** It's an adverb.

  They went **today. Today** tells **when.** It's an adverb.

  They went **slowly. Slowly** tells **how.** It's an adverb.

- Remember, if a word tells **where, when** or **how,** it's an adverb.

Part D

Sample Sentences

                V   N
1. The workers moved dirt.

                V   AV
2. The workers moved quickly.

Write the last two words and label the parts of speech: **V** for verb; **N** for noun; **AV** for adverb.

1. The dogs barked yesterday.
2. The girls looked east.
3. The scientists watched animals.
4. The cats went home.
5. My mother bought milk.
6. The hunters watched birds.
7. Her eyes looked up.
8. Tracy traveled alone.

| Copy the table and complete it so that each row is consistent.

Collections from Visuals Plus, Inc.

Collections	Cards	Stamps	Medallions	Price
Animals Unlimited	0	100	0	$10
Wild & Wilder	50	0	5	a.
Gold Medal Animals	100	200	10	b.
Peace World	0	0	15	$15
Endangered Species	150	0	0	$30
All Continent	c.	d.	e.	$60

Clues for consistency

✔ Figure out the cost of each **card** by dividing.

✔ Figure out the cost of each **stamp** by dividing.

✔ Figure out the cost of each **medallion** by dividing.

Part F   Follow the appropriate outline diagram to explain the problem with each argument.

Argument 1:   Bill goes to Readmore School, and he plays the piano. Sarah also goes to Readmore. I'll bet she's a good piano player.

Argument 2:   The Acme Factory did not produce many tires last month. Grace Peters works at Acme. She must not have done very much work last month.

Argument 3:   Jenny said that she has change for a quarter. Two dimes and a nickel is change for a quarter. Therefore, Jenny must have two dimes and a nickel.

Outline diagram

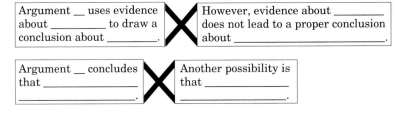

Part A | Write the last two words and label the parts of speech: **V** for verb; **N** for noun; **AV** for adverb.

1. The girls had adventures.
2. The ducks splashed water.
3. The puppies played vigorously.
4. The children sang songs.
5. The children sang loudly.
6. The dessert came later.
7. My uncle loves watermelons.
8. Hard exercises develop strength.

Part B | For one of the pictures, write the combined sentence. For the other picture, write just the **first sentence.**

Item 1:   The girl ran 4 miles. The girl wore number 17.

Item 2:   He painted the chair. The chair had a high back.

 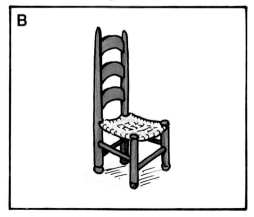

- Some sentences that refer to the present have **a part that tells about something that is always true.** When you change these sentences so they refer to the past, you don't change the verb for the part that is always true.

- Here's a sentence with a part that is always true:

    They discover that some rocks are hollow.

- Part of that sentence refers to something that is always true. That part says:

    Some rocks are hollow.

- You don't change the verb in that part when you rewrite the sentence:

    They discovered that some rocks are hollow.

- Remember, if part of the sentence tells about something that is always true, you don't change the verb in that part.

Part D | Rewrite each sentence so it refers to the past.

1. They notice that the squirrel is on their porch.
2. Jane is explaining why the sun sets in the west.
3. My younger brother is learning how hailstones form in clouds.
4. Our teacher explains that odd numbers cannot be divided by 2.
5. We are watching those shadows as the sun goes down.
6. Laura tells us that shadows always get longer as the sun goes down.

Follow the outline diagram to explain the inconsistencies in Table F12.

Table F12
Additional Collections from Visuals Plus, Inc.

Collection	Cards	Stamps	Medallions	Price
Our Favorite	10	10	10	$13
African Animals	20	0	20	$24
Global Life	100	100	0	$24

Outline diagram

_____ is not consistent with _____.

If _____ was consistent with _____, [tell about cost of collection]. [Tell why].

However, [tell about inconsistent collection] _____.

Independent Work

Part F | For each item, write the verb. Indicate the time: past, present or future.

1. Cathy will go with her mother.
2. A lot of rain fell last night.
3. Our cat has green eyes.
4. The mail carrier was running late.
5. Little Eddie found the hiding place.
6. They are working hard.

Argument 1:   Animals with eyes eat things.
Spiders have eyes.

                        [_____] .

Argument 2:   All of Jane's cats stayed out last night.
Little Missie is one of Jane's cats.

                        [_____] .

Argument 3:   Any number more than zero is a positive number.
Fourteen is a number that is more than zero.

                        [_____] .

Part A | Rewrite each sentence so it tells about the past.

We are preparing to do a science experiment. We want to find out which things float in water. Miss Richmond keeps telling us that objects more dense than water sink in water. Dennis thinks that some stones will float. I believe that he is wrong.

Part B

- You've worked with sentences that are already specific enough. These sentences do not need a part to make the meaning more specific; however, **you may add a part to these sentences.**

- Here's the rule about the added part:
  - ✔ If you **don't need** the part to make the meaning more specific, **you set the part off with commas** before and after the part.
  - ✔ If you **do need** the part to make the meaning more specific, **you do not use commas.**

- Here is the sentence with commas:

  Our neighbors, who live across the street, have a new car.

- Remember, if the part is not needed to make the sentence specific enough, you just set that part off with commas to show it is not needed.

Part C | Write the combined sentence for each item. Use commas to set off the part of the sentence that is not needed.

Item 1: The boy is always late.
The boy has short hair.

Item 2: The children played softball.
The children wore black T-shirts.

Here's the combined sentence:
The boy who has short hair is always late.

Part D | Write the combined sentence for each picture. Show the part that is not needed for one of the pictures by using commas.

The girl ran 3 miles. The girl wore number 17.

- Some sentences end with an adverb. Some end with an adjective.

- Here's how to test whether the last word is an adjective:

    Say the noun in the subject with the last word of the sentence in front of it. If what you say makes sense, the last word in the sentence is an adjective.

- Here's a sentence:

The vehicle was ⟨slow.⟩

- Here's the noun of the subject with the word **slow** in front of it:

slow vehicle

- That makes sense. **Slow** tells about the vehicle. So **slow** is an **adjective.**

- Here's another sentence:

The vehicle moved ⟨slowly.⟩

- Here's the noun of the subject with the word **slowly** in front of it:

slowly vehicle

- That does not make sense. So **slowly** is not an adjective. It's an **adverb.**

Write the last word of each sentence in front of the noun in the subject. Then label the part of speech: **N** for noun; **A** for adjective; **AV** for adverb.

1. The picture looked interesting.
2. The birds looked around.
3. The birds looked beautiful.
4. The work was difficult.
5. The shadows became longer.

6. The sun went down.
7. Five children came here.
8. Those sentences seem complicated.
9. Many birds flew together.
10. The workers felt tired.

Copy and complete the table. Fill in each blank so it is consistent with the other cars.

Table F13

Car	Number of functions for radio	Tires	Engine horsepower	Total cost
Spunky	2	basic	105 hp	$10,000
Hi Ride	10	a.	300 hp	$40,000
Rollo	b.	very good	200 hp	$30,000
Sleeko	4	good	150 hp	c.
Econo Car	d.	e.	99 hp	$8,800

Independent Work

Part H Complete each argument.

Argument 1:   All animals that do not have a backbone are called invertebrates.
A snail is an animal that does not have a backbone.

.

Argument 2:   As an object in the air gets closer to the surface of the earth, the pull of gravity on the object increases.
A spaceship is getting closer to the surface of the earth.

.

Use the chart and the outline diagram to write a paragraph about the differences between seagulls and penguins.

Chart

How Seagulls Are Different from Penguins

Facts about Seagulls	Facts about Penguins
large wings	small wings
light body	heavy body
can fly	can't fly

Outline diagram

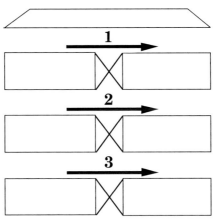

Lesson 34

- Some sentences tell the exact words that somebody said.
- The part that somebody said does not change whether the sentence tells about the past, the present or the future.
- Right now, Joe is saying, "My brother will go fishing on Friday."
- Yesterday, Joe said, "My brother will go fishing on Friday."
- Three days from now, Joe will say, "My brother will go fishing on Friday."
- Remember, the part of the sentence inside the quotation marks stays the same.

Part B | Rewrite the passage so it tells about the past.

Passage

Tim says, "We will wade across the stream."
Tina says, "We will get wet."
"We will take our shoes off," Tim replies.
Tim and Tina take off their shoes and wade across.

Part C | Write the last word of the sentence in front of the noun in the subject. Indicate the part of speech for each word.

1. The dog is unfriendly.
2. That dog growled fiercely.
3. The girls looked outside.
4. Those buildings look enormous.
5. The snow fell softly.
6. His argument seemed good.
7. The groups worked together.
8. The children cheered loudly.
9. The children were loud.

Write the combined sentence for each picture. Show the part that is not needed for one of the pictures by using commas.

Item 1: The woman is from Chicago. The woman sat next to Marty.

Item 2: The players played poorly. The players wore black uniforms.

Item 3: The woman drives fast. The woman wears sneakers.

Use the table and the outline diagram to write two paragraphs that describe the inconsistent features—one about Bumpo cars and one about Stampo cars.

Table F13

Car	Number of functions for radio	Tires	Engine horsepower	Total cost
Spunky	2	basic	105 hp	$10,000
Hi Ride	10		300 hp	$40,000
Rollo		very good	200 hp	$30,000
Sleeko	4	good	150 hp	
Econo Car			99 hp	$8,800
Bumpo	**10**	**super deluxe**	**120 hp**	**$48,000**
Stampo	**2**	**super deluxe**	**100 hp**	**$9,400**

Outline diagram

___[feature(s)]___ (is/are) not consistent with the price of the car.

The car costs _____. If the ___[feature(s)]___ (was/were) consistent with the price, ___[feature(s)]___ would _____ _____.

However, ___[feature(s)]___ (is/are) _____ _____.

Part F | Rewrite each sentence that has a silly meaning.

1. Vern worked harder than the other workers.
2. Emily liked spiders better than anybody else in her family.
3. The snakes moved faster than the gophers.
4. Our garage was dirtier than our basement.
5. The truck held a lot more than our trailer.
6. They carried more from the house than the shed.
7. Inez collected more spiders than beetles.

Part G | Follow the outline diagram to describe how you would test the rule.

Rule: Something that is made out of aluminum weighs less than the same thing made out of steel.

Outline diagram

To test the rule, you could ___[how much]___
_____.

If _____
_____,
the evidence would
discredit the rule.

If _____
_____,
the evidence would
not discredit the rule.

Lesson  35

Part A   If both parts are essential, write a combined sentence with no
commas. If the second part is not essential, set it off with commas.

1. *Here's the essential part of what you want to say:*
   His mother drives very slowly.
   Here's the part you want to add:
   She wears glasses.

2. *Here's the essential part of what you want to say:*
   The boy got good grades in school.
   Here's another essential part:
   That boy lives next door.

3. *Here's the essential part of what you want to say:*
   He had an argument with his oldest sister.
   Here's the part you want to add:
   His oldest sister is an excellent athlete.

4. *Here's the essential part of what you want to say:*
   He gave 12 dollars to the girl.
   Here's another essential part:
   That girl was selling tickets.

5. *Here's the essential part of what you want to say:*
   He talked with Maude.
   Here's the part you want to add:
   Maude lives on the next block.

Part B

- You have learned to test nouns and adjectives that are at the end of sentences.

- You test nouns by figuring out if you can replace the word with a pronoun. If you can, the word you are testing is a noun.

- You test adjectives by seeing if the word you're testing makes sense in front of a noun.

- Here's a sentence:

My sister will visit tomorrow.

- **Tomorrow** may be a noun, an adverb or an adjective.

- We test to see if it's a noun. We can't replace it with a pronoun that means **tomorrow,** so **tomorrow** is not a noun.

- Now we test to see if it's an adjective. We say **sister** with **tomorrow** in front of it: **tomorrow sister.**

- That doesn't make sense. So **tomorrow** is not an adjective. **Tomorrow** is an adverb.

Part C | Write the last word of each sentence and indicate the part of speech.

1. My sister will visit Henry.
2. My sister visits often.
3. My sister is friendly.
4. My sister gets nervous.
5. My sister gets rashes.
6. My sister stays inside.
7. My sister washes clothes.
8. My sister washes often.

Part D

- Sometimes the subject of a sentence has a possessive word that is shown with an apostrophe.

- Here's the rule about most of those words:

    You read the part that appears before the apostrophe. That tells you whether the sentence refers to **one** or **more than one.**

- Here are two sentences:

    1. **The car's brakes are worn.**
    2. **The cars' brakes are worn.**

- Sentence 1 tells about the brakes of **one car.** Sentence 2 tells about the brakes of **more than one car.**

- Remember, find the part before the apostrophe. That part tells you if the sentence refers to one or more than one.

Part E

Sample Sentences

A. The sunset's color was red.

B. The bricks' color was red.

For each item, write **one** or **more than one.** Tell the name of the thing that is one or more than one.

1. The boys' boats were in the water.
2. The clown's balloon was huge.
3. The dogs' howling frightened the scouts.
4. The groups' grade was very high.
5. My brothers' dog did amazing tricks.
6. The rock's weight was more than 80 pounds.
7. The stars' brilliance was amazing.
8. The ship's guns were silent.

Part F

- Two punctuation marks that you use when you write related sentences arc thc **colon** and the **semicolon.**

- Here's a **colon:** :

- Here's a **semicolon:** ;

- The **colon** is sometimes used to introduce a series of sentences. The **semicolon** may be used between the sentences that follow.

- Here's an example:

    The report indicated the following: The car struck the guardrail at 3:14 a.m.; the car then skidded 68 feet; and it came to rest under the 12th Street bridge.

Part G

- Some reports are inconsistent. They may be true, but they raise serious questions.

- Here's an inconsistent report:

    The Human Fly struck again on Saturday at 6:32 a.m. He walked right up to the side of the Bank Tower Building and immediately began to climb.

    He went straight up the smooth glass wall with no visible means of support. His hands were bare and empty, but they seemed to stick to the wall like powerful magnets. Also, his feet, which were clad in ordinary sneakers, had a remarkable magnetic power.

    It took the Human Fly only about 20 minutes to reach the top, and then he disappeared without a trace.

    No witnesses saw the Human Fly climb the Bank Tower Building. The police are therefore anxious to talk to anyone who saw these events. Police are beginning to wonder if the Human Fly is a normal person or someone with superhuman powers.

Follow the outline diagram to write about the inconsistent report in part G.

Outline diagram

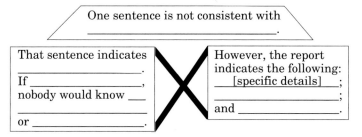

One sentence is not consistent with
_____.

That sentence indicates
_____.
If _____,
nobody would know ___
_____
or _____.

However, the report
indicates the following:
____[specific details]____;
_____;
and _____.

Independent Work

Part I

Follow the outline diagram to describe how you would test the rule.

Rule: Very hot glass breaks when you drop it in cold water.

Outline diagram

To test the rule, you could ___[how much]___
_____.

If _____
_____,
the evidence would
discredit the rule.

If _____
_____,
the evidence would
not discredit the rule.

Part J

Copy each sentence and label the parts of speech.

1. She kissed her mother.
2. I followed John.
3. Her eyes looked up.
4. The picture looked beautiful.

Lesson 36

Part A

For each sentence, write the last word and indicate the part of speech.

1. My cat eats frequently.
2. My cat eats fish.
3. My cat is gray.
4. My cat went out.

5. My cat jumps around.
6. My cat sleeps there.
7. My cat chases mice.
8. My cat looks sleepy.

Part B

For each item, write **one** or **more than one** with the appropriate name.

1. The computers' power supply failed.
2. The boat's engines made a terrible noise.
3. The animal's tricks amazed the crowd.
4. The students' paper was well written.
5. The girls' notebooks fell off the shelf.
6. My cousins' clothes got very muddy.

- You've used the word **that** in combined sentences.
- Here's the rule:
  - ✔ You use the word **that** when the part that is added is **essential**.
  - ✔ You replace the word **that** with the word **which** if the part is **not essential**.
- Here are two pictures and two sentences.

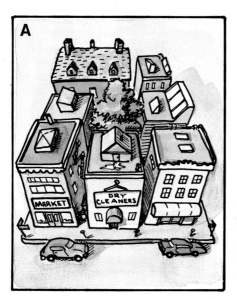 

We went to the market <u>that is next to the dry cleaners</u>.

- The underlined part of that sentence is essential.

  We went to the market, <u>which is next to the dry cleaners</u>.

- The underlined part of that sentence is not essential. It is set off with a comma, and it begins with the word **which**, not **that**.

For each item, write the combined sentence.

1. *Here's an essential part:*
   She has an old bike.
   Here's a part you want to add:
   The bike is red and white.

2. *Here's an essential part:*
   She has an old bike.
   Here's another essential part:
   That bike is red and white.

3. *Here's an essential part:*
   She wanted to buy a camera.
   Here's another essential part:
   That camera cost $450.

4. *Here's an essential part:*
   Her camera takes wonderful pictures.
   Here's a part you want to add:
   That camera is on sale at Z-Mart.

5. *Here's an essential part:*
   That train gets here at 6 a.m.
   Here's a part you want to add:
   That train comes from Chicago.

Clarence Build went to a doctor because he was experiencing a lot of stress. Here's part of what he told the doctor:

> One of the things that bothers me is the poor workmanship on my new summer home. For a house that cost $350,000, it has a lot of little things that are not top quality. Also, the car I bought last month is a disappointment. That car cost over $48,000 and yet it has an engine with only 120 horsepower. The two gardeners that work at my winter home are another problem. They are always asking for more money. They think they should be paid more than $10 an hour. And they only want to work five days a week. That's ridiculous because I don't make more than $10 an hour. I have to work on Saturdays, too, but I don't complain.

Outline diagram

One sentence is not _____
_____.

That sentence indicates
_____.
If _____,
he could not _____
_____ or _____
_____.

However, the report indicates the following:
_____;
_____;
and _____.
[Be specific.]

Part F Follow the outline diagram to tell about the best car choice for Mr. Nelson.

Mr. Nelson's requirements for a car

1. The car must cost under $15,000.
2. The car must be able to hold 5 people.
3. The car must have at least 9 cubic feet of storage space.
4. The car must have at least 160 horsepower.

Facts

Car	Engine	Storage capacity	Seating capacity	Cost
Dupol	260 horsepower	9 cubic feet	6 adults	$31,200
Bumpo	103 horsepower	0 cubic feet	3 adults	$15,000
Eneet	180 horsepower	11 cubic feet	6 adults	$15,600
Cheapo	120 horsepower	3 cubic feet	5 adults	$7,999

Outline diagram

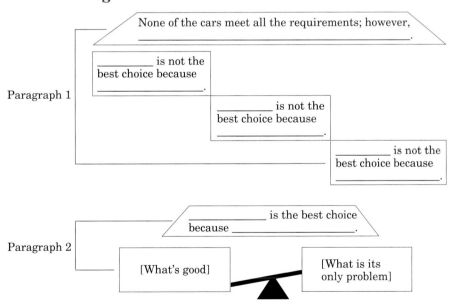

None of the cars meet all the requirements; however, _____.

Paragraph 1

_____ is not the best choice because _____.

_____ is not the best choice because _____.

_____ is not the best choice because _____.

_____ is the best choice because _____.

Paragraph 2

[What's good]

[What is its only problem]

Lesson 37

Part A

> Write **Part A** in the left margin of your paper and number it from 1 to 12. Read the passage and study the table below. Then write the answers to the questions.

Passage

On Monday morning, Ms. Hassel returned English and math tests to her class and explained her grading system.

Here's a summary: One hundred points were possible.

Fifty points were possible on the math test.

Fifty points were possible on the English test.

A student had to earn at least 30 points to pass each part

A student needed a total score of 70 points to pass the test.

Two students did not pass the English test.

All students passed the math test.

The hardest part was the editing part of the English test. Many students left words misspelled, and the students were weak on placing commas appropriately.

Students who did well all year on the homework assignments did well on the tests.

Two students who did little or no homework also did well on the tests.

The two students who scored less than 30 on the English test will spend some extra time with the teacher this week. They will take the test again on Friday.

Student	Math	English	Total	Absent
1. Alvin	36	48	84	
2. Owen	42	29	71	
3. Kim	50	35	85	
4. Frank				x
5. Sharon	46	45	91	
6. Rainbow	41	39	80	
7. Tofu	37	33	70	
8. Henry	49	47	96	
9. Joseph	33	24	57	
10. Brian	46	42	88	
11. Cecily				x
12. Marilyn	44	41	85	
13. Laurie	48	45	93	
14. James	50	49	99	
15. Peter	41	43	84	
16. Martha	39	37	76	
17. Nancy	43	39	82	
18. David	46	41	87	
19. Leroy	37	39	76	
20. Candice	41	42	83	
21. Mary	50	49	99	
22. Nickolas	48	42	90	
23. Mick	39	34	73	
24. Tina	49	38	77	
25. Regina	45	40	75	

Part A continued

Some of the questions below ask where you found the answer. Use this key:

- Write **P** if the answer is found in the passage.
- Write **T** if the answer is found in the table.
- Write **PT** if the answer is found in both the passage and the table.

1. How many points are possible on the entire test?
2. Where would somebody find the answer to question 1?

3. Does the English test or the math test have the higher possible score?
4. Where would somebody find the answer to question 3?

5. Did more students pass the English part of the test or the math part?
6. Where would somebody find the answer to question 5?

7. How many students took the test?
8. Where would somebody find the answer to question 7?

9. How many students were absent?
10. Where would somebody find the answer to question 9?

11. How many students scored less than 30 on the English part of the test?
12. Where would somebody find the answer to question 11?

1. *Here's an essential part:*
   The chair was in our garage.
   Here's a part you want to add:
   The chair had a broken leg.

2. *Here's an essential part:*
   The chair was in our garage.
   Here's another essential part:
   The chair had a broken leg.

3. *Here's an essential part:*
   The store is on the corner.
   Here's another essential part:
   The store sells mountain bikes.

4. *Here's an essential part:*
   The truck won't start.
   Here's a part you want to add:
   The truck is parked in the alley.

5. *Here's an essential part:*
   We completed the test.
   Here's a part you want to add:
   The test had 50 items.

6. *Here's an essential part:*
   We bought hammers.
   Here's another essential part:
   The hammers were on sale.

Copy each sentence. Indicate the part of speech for each word.

1. Five girls came here.
2. Green butterflies are rare.
3. Some boys are energetic.
4. Those young women teach engineers.
5. The delivery person is late.
6. Her dad speaks often.
7. Your oldest sister left yesterday.
8. Their document presented information.

Part D

Mona Lisa

Vocabulary Box

Leonardo da Vinci	Italy	Paris
detectives	France	

Part E | Follow the outline diagram to tell about the best car choice for Ms. Carlson.

Ms. Carlson's requirements for a car

1. The car must get at least 6,000 miles between oil changes.
2. The car must get at least 30 miles per gallon.
3. The car must cost under $20,000.
4. The car must be able to hold at least 3 adults.
5. The car must have at least 140 horsepower.

Facts

Car	Engine	Storage capacity	Seating capacity	Cost	Miles between oil changes	Gas mileage
Dupol	260 horsepower	9 cubic feet	6 adults	$31,200	20,000	18 miles per gallon
Bumpo	103 horsepower	0 cubic feet	3 adults	$15,000	6,000	17 miles per gallon
Eneet	180 horsepower	11 cubic feet	6 adults	$15,600	5,000	31 miles per gallon
Cheapo	120 horsepower	3 cubic feet	5 adults	$7,999	4,000	46 miles per gallon

Outline diagram

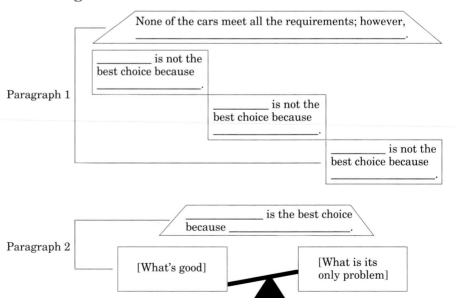

None of the cars meet all the requirements; however, _____.

Paragraph 1

_____ is not the best choice because _____.

_____ is not the best choice because _____.

_____ is not the best choice because _____.

Paragraph 2

_____ is the best choice because _____.

[What's good]   [What is its only problem]

Lesson 38

| For each item, write the combined sentence.

1. *Here's an essential part:*
   They finally fixed the antenna.
   Here's a part you want to add:
   The antenna is on the garage roof.

2. *Here's an essential part:*
   His brother drives very fast.
   Here's another essential part:
   His brother lives in California.

3. *Here's an essential part:*
   The girl lives on a farm.
   Here's another essential part:
   The girl bought our dog.

4. *Here's an essential part:*
   I was baking bread.
   Here's a part you want to add:
   The bread rises in 30 minutes.

5. *Here's an essential part:*
   Andy is going to visit me in December.
   Here's a part you want to add:
   Andy has been my friend for years.

Part B | Copy each sentence. Indicate the part of speech for each word.

1. The horse was awkward.

2. Those white birds are doves.

3. Billy swims well.

4. Our six candles burned quickly.

5. That stove burns logs.

6. Chimneys gather soot.

7. Our assignment was difficult.

Part C | Rewrite each sentence so it has the word **of.**

> **Sample Sentence**
> The boat's engines made a racket.
> **Rewritten sentence:**
> The engines of the boat made a racket.

1. The chimneys' smoke covered the city.

2. The rabbit's paws were pink.

3. The tree's colors changed quickly.

4. The groups' arguments sounded confusing.

Part D | Write **Part D** in the left margin of your paper. Then number from 1 to 10. Read the passage below and write the answers to the questions.

Passage

The flooding began after several days of unusually rainy weather. The Green River was swollen with water from the many smaller streams and canals that feed it. Water first spilled over the banks in a farming area near Harper and washed out some early plantings of corn and beans. Some sheep and cattle had to be herded to higher ground, but there was not yet any threat to people.

The rains didn't stop during the next week. More and more farmland went under water, and then levees and dams all along the river began to fail. Water just poured over the tops of some levees. Others broke or were washed completely away. Roadways flooded; bridges collapsed; and the water began to rise in the big cities downriver.

People in the cities put up a good fight at first. They filled millions of sandbags and piled them against the rising water, but the fight was mostly in vain. Everywhere, the river broke through. Water poured into the streets and flooded stores, schools, restaurants and thousands of homes.

Residents along the river could do nothing but flee. The water came up so fast that many had to leave with only the clothes they were wearing. It was fully two weeks before people could return to their homes.

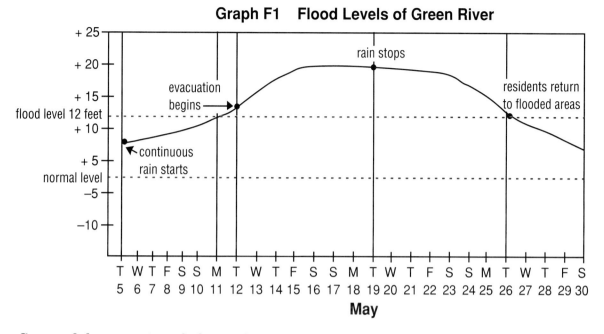

Graph F1   Flood Levels of Green River

Some of the questions below ask where you found the answer. Use this key:

- Write **P** if the answer is found in the passage.
- Write **G** if the answer is found in the graph.
- Write **PG** if the answer is found in both the passage and the graph.

1. On what day of the week did the river go above flooding level?
2. Where would somebody find the answer to question 1?

3. Where did the flooding begin?
4. Where would somebody find the answer to question 3?

5. How many feet above normal is flood stage?
6. Where would somebody find the answer to question 5?

7. What is the name of the river?
8. Where would somebody find the answer to question 7?

9. How many days after the rain stopped did people return to their homes?
10. Where would somebody find the answer to question 9?

Part E | Follow the outline diagram to tell about the best car choice for Jan.

Jan's requirements for a car

1. The car must hold 6 adults.
2. The car must have a storage capacity of more than 7 cubic feet.
3. The car must have more than 300 horsepower.
4. The car must go 20,000 miles between oil changes.
5. The car must get more than 17 miles per gallon.

Facts

Car	Engine	Storage capacity	Seating capacity	Cost	Miles between oil changes	Gas mileage
Dupol	260 horsepower	9 cubic feet	6 adults	$31,200	20,000	18 miles per gallon
Bumpo	103 horsepower	0 cubic feet	3 adults	$15,000	6,000	17 miles per gallon
Eneet	180 horsepower	11 cubic feet	6 adults	$15,600	5,000	31 miles per gallon
Cheapo	120 horsepower	3 cubic feet	5 adults	$7,999	4,000	46 miles per gallon

Outline diagram

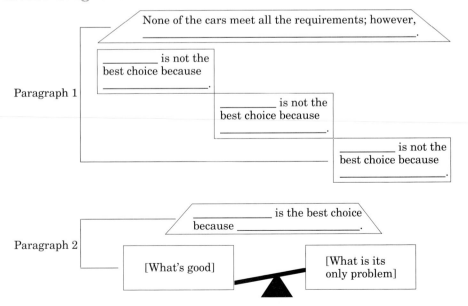

Lesson 39

Part A Rewrite each sentence so it has the word **of.**

1. The birds' songs were interesting.
2. The boys' interests were unusual.
3. The waters' color was brilliant.
4. The conclusions' wording was confusing.
5. The forest's smells were strong.

Part B
- You've worked with passages that are inconsistent. They are not necessarily false, but they have parts that raise serious questions about the other parts.

- One passage you read was about the Human Fly. That passage was not necessarily false. But how would it be possible for the reporter to know what the Human Fly did if there were no witnesses?

- You read a passage about Mr. Build and his possessions. How would it be possible for him to earn only 10 dollars an hour and have all the things he has?

Passage A

The report on the Human Fly failed to indicate how the police knew what the Fly did, how he did it, and when he accomplished his remarkable feat. The answer is a video camera. The Bank Tower Building has an automatic alarm system that sets off cameras. The moment the Human Fly started scaling the wall, a camera recorded everything he did. The camera indicated the time that he started. It clearly showed him climbing the wall with bare hands and wearing ordinary sneakers. The facts reported were accurate. He started climbing the wall at 6:22 a.m. He reached the top 20 minutes later, and then he disappeared.

Passage B

Mr. Build's doctor was shocked when Build indicated that he earned no more than 10 dollars an hour. The doctor pointed out that people with such earnings do not own lavish summer homes or employ two gardeners. Mr. Build pointed out that his grandfather had died three years before and had left Mr. Build approximately 41 million dollars.

Part D

- Some accounts are **inconsistent.** They are not necessarily false because it may be possible to explain the details that are inconsistent.

- Other accounts are **contradictory** because it's not possible for all their information to be true.

- Here's an example:

    Mr. Matsui left work at 5:06 p.m. He took the train home, and he arrived at his house at 5:09 p.m.

For each item, write **inconsistent** or **contradictory.**

Item 1: Bonnie finished in fourth place in the 100-meter dash. When she got home, she proudly presented her mother with the medal that she received for first place.

Item 2: Farmer Smith has a 100-acre farm. Her next door neighbor has a 20-acre farm. Both plant the same crops every year; however, Farmer Jones always harvests over twice the amount that Farmer Smith harvests.

Item 3: On Friday the 14th, the sky was cloudless and the moon was a sliver. Three days later, however, we danced under a full moon.

Item 4: Mr. Singh has only three types of animals on his ranch. They are saddle horses, goats and cattle. Recently, Mr. Singh started having a lot of trouble with his horses. Many of them have been injured by tripping over gopher holes, which appeared all over the ranch.

Follow the outline diagram to write about the contradiction in Jimmy's report.

Jimmy's report

Jimmy borrowed Eddie's lawnmower. When Jimmy returned it, Eddie noticed that the blade was badly damaged, and the lawnmower wouldn't run.

He said, "Jimmy, this blade was in good condition when you borrowed the lawnmower. Now it's broken. You must have done something to break it."

Jimmy said, "No. When I used the lawnmower, I just mowed my front yard. I didn't run over any rocks or anything that could damage the blade. Also, it was running perfectly when I was done using it."

"That's strange," Eddie said.

Jimmy said, "And besides, the blade was already broken when I borrowed the lawnmower."

Outline diagram

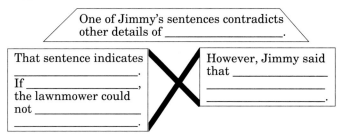

Copy each sentence. Write letters to show the parts of speech for all the words.

1. My brother runs fast.
2. His sister is pretty.
3. Those boxes hold cups.
4. Seven curious ducks looked around.
5. The neighbors argued loudly.

Part G | Write the letter of the picture each sentence refers to.

1. The boy stood next to the store that had a cracked window.

2. The boy who was wearing a cap stood next to the store.

3. The boy stood next to the store, which had a cracked window.

4. The boy, who was wearing a cap, stood next to the store.

For each item, write the combined sentence using **who, that** or **which.** Punctuate the combined sentences correctly.

1. *This part is essential:*
   The girl was getting sick.
   This part is essential:
   That girl wore a black coat.

2. *This part is essential:*
   The rug has many fleas in it.
   This part is not essential:
   That rug belongs in the hall.

3. *This part is essential:*
   A tree fell on a car.
   This part is essential:
   The car was in our driveway.

4. *This part is essential:*
   The girls picked flowers.
   This part is not essential:
   The flowers were red.

Part A

Write a value for each box that has missing information. The value must be **consistent** with the other information in the table.

> **Here are some general rules:**
> 1. Lighter bikes cost more.
> 2. Quick-change wheels cost more.
> 3. More gears cost more.

Bike	Weight	Wheels	Number of gears	Price
Winner I	30 pounds	regular	12	$200
Winner II	30 pounds	quick change	12	$500
Miler	17 pounds	a.	27	$1,500
Fleet-Go	25 pounds	quick change	15	b.
Super B	24 pounds	c.	16	$900
Bumbo	32 pounds	regular	12	d.
Primo	e.	f.	g.	$1,600

Part B

Copy the last word in each sentence. Write the letter to show the part of speech.

1. The dogs followed rabbits.
2. The dogs moved slowly.
3. The dogs were tired.
4. The dogs got wet.
5. The dogs howled again.

Part C | Rewrite each sentence so it has the word **of.**

1. The girls' hair was wet.
2. They listened to the doctor's instructions.
3. I listened to the birds' singing.
4. The mountain's colors were changing.

Part D | For each item, write the combined sentence using **who, that** or **which.** Punctuate the combined sentences correctly.

1. *This part is essential:*
   The man delivered pizza.
   This part is not essential:
   The man wore suspenders.

2. *This part is essential:*
   The posts had nails in them.
   This part is essential:
   Those posts were in Mr. Green's yard.

3. *This part is essential:*
   We examined a roof.
   This part is not essential:
   The roof was red and black.

4. *This part is essential:*
   The breeze came from the north.
   This part is not essential:
   That breeze felt delightful.

Part A | Rewrite each sentence so it has the word **of.**

1. The gardens' odor filled the air.
2. The boy's hands were cold.
3. The trains' wheels screeched as they stopped.
4. The bee's wings hummed.
5. The streets' surface was worn.
6. The bird's songs were interesting.

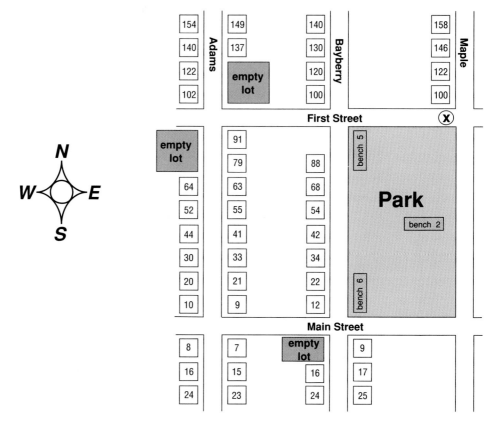

Directions: Go west on First Street.
Turn at Adams.
Go to the fourth house on your left.

Outline diagram

The directions are not specific enough.

If you followed the directions, you would go to
_____ or _____.

Directions for going to
_____ would say,
"_____."

Directions for going to
_____ would say,
"_____."

- Some sentences with parts that are not essential explain the meaning of unfamiliar words.

- Here's a sentence:

  They went on board a galleon.

- The word **galleon** may be unfamiliar to the reader. So the sentence may be rewritten to include a part that explains what a **galleon** is:

  They went on board a galleon, which is a type of large sailing ship used in the years 1400 through 1700.

- Notice that the part that is added starts with the words **which is** and tells about the main features of a galleon. It tells what a galleon is—a **ship.** It also tells how it is different from other ships. A galleon is a **sailing** ship, and it was used in the years 1400 through 1700.

Part D | For each item, use a dictionary and rewrite the sentence so it explains what the uncommon word means.

1. She rode a handsome Appaloosa.

2. Many European people enjoy borscht.

3. Everybody laughed over the clown's hoodoo.

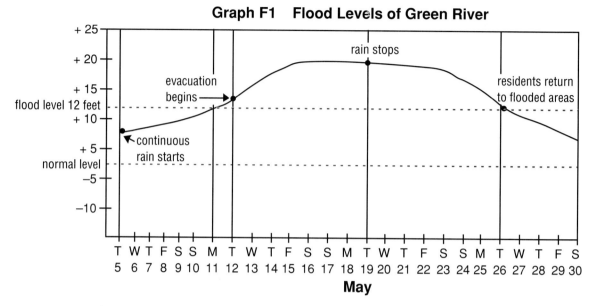

Graph F1   Flood Levels of Green River

Account

The rain started on May 5th and stopped on May 19th. After four days of heavy rain, people had to evacuate their houses. The level of the water reached flooding stage on May 11th and stayed in the flood range until May 26th. People returned home on May 27th.

Outline diagram

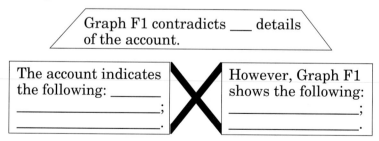

Graph F1 contradicts ___ details of the account.

The account indicates the following: _____
_____ ;
_____ .

However, Graph F1 shows the following:
_____ ;
_____ .

Part F

- Some verbs are **is** verbs.
- Those verbs include: **are, was, were, is** and **am.**
- Here are sentences with **is** verbs:

  > **They** were **tired.**
  > **She** is **hungry.**
  > **Those girls** are **hard workers.**
  > **I** am **happy.**

- Each sentence has one-word verb. If a sentence has one of these verbs **and an action word,** the sentence does not have an **is** verb.
- None of these sentences has an **is** verb:

  > **She** runs.
  > **She** is running.
  > **My uncles** were collecting **papers.**
  > **The butterflies** fly.
  > **The butterflies** are flying.
  > **I** am thinking **about things.**

- Remember, if a sentence has the words **is, are, was, were** or **am** and has no other verb word, the verb is an **is** verb.

Part G | Write the verb of each sentence. Circle it if it is an **is** verb.

1. The girls ran fast.
2. The girls were running fast.
3. The two boys were playing catch.
4. The two boys were cousins.
5. The cans are rolling downhill.
6. Those dogs are sitting near my house.
7. The cans are red and white.
8. I am running for class president.
9. Susan was asking about the election.
10. I am a good student.

Part H | For each item, write a combined sentence that uses **who, which** or **that.** Punctuate the sentences correctly.

1. *Here's a part that is essential:*
   That girl fell off her bike.
   Here's a part that is not essential:
   The girl lives in the red house on the corner.

2. *Here's a part that is essential:*
   They went to the bank.
   Here's a part that is essential:
   The bank is next to the fairgrounds.

3. *Here's a part that is essential:*
   They bought a new car.
   Here's a part that is not essential:
   The car gets very good mileage.

4. *Here's a part that is essential:*
   Witnesses identified the person.
   Here's a part that is essential:
   That person robbed the bank.

5. *Here's a part that is essential:*
   They received a lot of money.
   Here's a part that is not essential:
   That money came from the sale of fish.

6. *Here's a part that is essential:*
   Nick loves the pizza.
   Here's a part that is essential:
   The pizza comes from Tony's Restaurant.

Write the last word in each sentence. Indicate the part of speech: **AV** for adverb; **A** for adjective; **N** for noun.

1. She was beautiful.
2. The fish jumped often.
3. Our building is wooden.
4. Jim purchased goods.
5. All my cousins are carpenters.
6. Andy collected wood.
7. Those boats were light.
8. Our neighbors shopped late.
9. I turned off the light.

Lesson 42

Part A | For each item, write the verb. If the verb is a form of **is,** circle it.

1. My sister was sleeping.
2. The girls are ready.
3. Five dogs stand on our porch.
4. Those dogs were nervous.
5. I am riding my bike.
6. I am in a hurry.
7. The crickets were near the pond.
8. The crickets were making noise.
9. He asks many questions.

Follow the outline diagram to write about the problems with the directions.

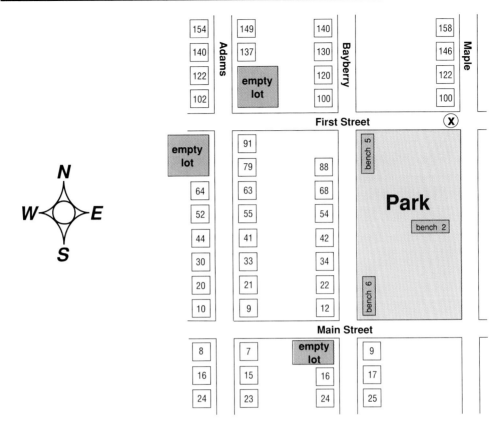

Directions: Go west on First Street.
Turn south.
Go to the house on your right that is just before
Main Street.

Outline diagram

The directions are not specific enough.

If you followed the directions, you would go to
_____ or _____ .

Directions for going to
_____ would say,
"_____ ."

Directions for going to
_____ would say,
"_____ ."

For each item, use a dictionary and rewrite the sentence so it explains what the uncommon word means.

1. Emily said that Mrs. Sanchez's dog reminded her of a knackwurst.

2. Horace was very good with a cant hook.

3. Kurt had fond memories of the pampas.

Part D

- Here's information about some adjectives and adverbs: You can change some adjectives into adverbs by adding the letters **ly** to the end of the word.

  The word **beautiful** is an adjective.

  The word **beautifully** is an adverb.

  The word **slow** is an adjective.

  The word **slowly** is an adverb.

- Some sentences end with an adjective. Some end with an adverb.

- Here are the rules for using the appropriate part of speech for the last word:

  ✔ If the sentence has an **is** verb, the correct word at the end of the sentence is an **adjective.**

  ✔ If the sentence does **not** have an **is** verb, the correct word at the end of the sentence is an **adverb.**

- Here's a pair of sentences that are correct:

  The animal was quick.

  The animal was moving quickly.

- The first sentence has an **is** verb. The sentences ends with an adjective.

- The second sentence does **not** have an **is** verb. The sentence ends with an adverb.

Part E

Sample Sentences	A. The girls danced _____ . B. The girls were _____ .	beautiful

Complete each sentence with the correct adjective or adverb.

1. a. He was talking _____ .
   b. He was _____ . | loud |

2. a. The bug was _____ .
   b. The bug moved _____ . | slow |

3. a. They walk _____ .
   b. They are _____ . | quick |

4. a. Our friend dresses _____ .
   b. Our friend is _____ . | careful |

5. a. He is _____ .
   b. He is driving _____ . | careless |

Follow the outline diagram to write a paragraph that describes the contradictions in the account and the graph.

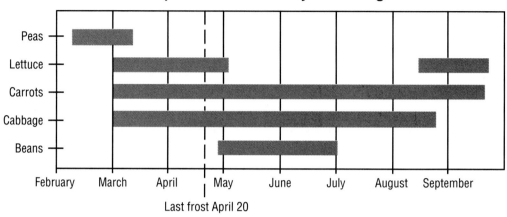

Graph F2 Carrot County Gardening Chart

Last frost April 20

Account

In Carrot County, your soil is good, and you have plenty of water. So you can grow anything.

Because you're close to the ocean, winter never gets too cold, and the growing season starts early. In February, even if there's still snow on the ground, start planting peas. Some people say you can start lettuce this early, too, but it's better to wait until March for that. In any case, it never freezes after the first week of March, so you can get a good jump on many other crops as well.

Carrots and cabbage both do well from March through midsummer, and cabbage can keep producing all summer long and into the fall. Beans should be started after the last frost date. If you start your tomatoes indoors and transplant them after the soil warms up, you can enjoy sweet ripe fruits from the Fourth of July until Halloween.

Outline diagram

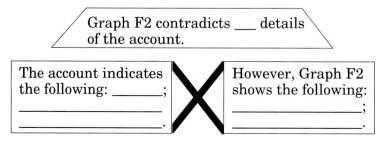

Graph F2 contradicts ___ details of the account.

The account indicates the following: _____;
_____
_____.

However, Graph F2 shows the following:
_____
_____;
_____.

Part G | All of these items are inconsistent, not contradictory. Follow the outline diagram and explain how each inconsistency is possible.

1. Ted's grandmother is nearly 80 years old. She is very, very intelligent. She told Ted that by next year she would finish high school.

2. Dan weighed 220 pounds with all his clothes on. Without his clothes, he weighed 150 pounds.

Outline diagram

> Possibly, _____.
> [Tell more if necessary.]

Part H | Rewrite each sentence so it has the word **of.**

1. The birds' song was loud.
2. The bird's song was loud.
3. My cousin's habits are disgusting.
4. My cousins' habits are disgusting.
5. The girl's tents were yellow.
6. The girls' dresses were yellow.
7. The girl's brother was mean.

Lesson 43

Part A | Complete each sentence with the correct adjective or adverb.

1. a. Her voice was _____ .
   b. She was speaking _____ . |quiet|

2. a. The engine was _____ .
   b. The engine started up _____ . |loud|

3. a. They spell very _____ .
   b. Their spelling is _____ . |poor|

4. a. She was singing _____ .
   b. Her singing voice was _____ . |soft|

5. a. Those spiders are very _____ .
   b. The spiders move _____ . |quick|

Part B

northwest [   ] northeast

southwest [   ] southeast

N
W ◇ E
S

Follow the outline diagram to write about the problems with the directions.

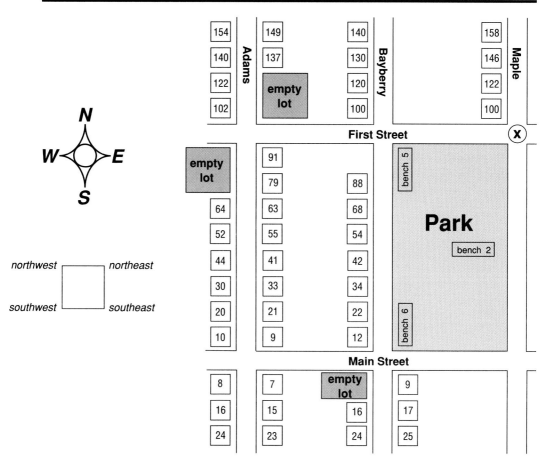

Directions A: Go to the bench that is on the west side of park.

Directions B: Go south to Main Street.
Then go to the house that is directly across the street from the southwest corner of the park.

Outline diagram

Directions __ are not specific enough.

If you followed the directions, you would go to _____ or _____.

Directions for going to _____ would say,
" _____ ."

Directions for going to _____ would say,
" _____ ."

Part C For each item, use a dictionary and rewrite the sentence so it explains what the uncommon word means.

1. Dr. Johnson went to ancient communities to study facades.

2. A duiker darted over the hill.

3. Leverets must be aware of hawks.

Account 1

The Human Fly struck again on Saturday at 6:32 a.m. He walked right up to the side of the Bank Tower Building and immediately began to climb.

He went up the smooth glass wall with no visible means of support. His hands were bare and empty, but they seemed to stick to the wall like powerful magnets. Also, his feet, which were clad in ordinary sneakers, had a remarkable magnetic power.

It took the Human Fly only about 20 minutes to reach the top, and then he disappeared without a trace.

No witnesses saw the Human Fly climb the Bank Tower Building. The police are therefore anxious to talk to anyone who saw these events. Police are beginning to wonder if the Human Fly is a normal person or someone with superhuman powers.

Account 2

Police are still searching for the daring and athletic person known as the Human Fly, who has now made six appearances this year. The Fly took advantage of sleeping guards and scaled downtown's Bank Tower early Saturday morning.

Although several local buildings are taller, none is smoother than the Bank Tower. Police are guessing that its perfect glass wall presented a special challenge to the Fly, who climbed to the top in exactly half an hour.

Six witnesses say that the feat was performed without any special equipment. Witnesses agreed that the climber had no ropes or harnesses for security, that his hands were bare, and that he wore regular sneakers on his feet. Shortly after he reached the top, police arrived on the scene and surrounded the building, but somehow the Human Fly escaped without leaving a trace.

Outline diagram

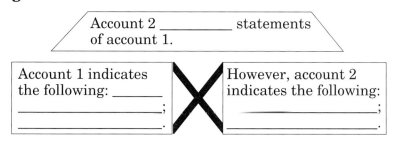

Account 2 _____ statements of account 1.

Account 1 indicates the following: _____
_____;
_____.

However, account 2 indicates the following:
_____;
_____.

Part E | For each item, write the combined sentence that uses **who, that** or **which.** Punctuate the sentences correctly.

1. *This part is essential:*
   The old man rescued the girl.
   This part is not essential:
   The old man always wears running shoes.

2. *This part is essential:*
   My doctor takes lots of vacations.
   This part is not essential:
   She lives in Bloomfield.

3. *This part is essential:*
   They had fun on their vacation.
   This part is not essential:
   The vacation lasted 24 days.

4. *This part is essential:*
   The dog is very mean.
   This part is essential:
   The dog has a scar on his nose.

5. *This part is essential:*
   Their neighbor plays his radio all the time.
   This part is essential:
   That neighbor lives just south of them.

Follow the outline diagram to write about the problem with each argument.

Argument 1: Mrs. Anderson's class is very noisy. Wanda is in that classroom. She must be a very noisy child.

Argument 2: Lisa is a member of the Summer Club, and she is a super swimmer. Wayne is also a member of the Summer Club. He must swim as well as Lisa.

Argument 3: Bombs are very bad because they kill people. Bombs are made of metal. Therefore, metal is a bad material.

Outline diagram

Argument __ uses evidence about _____ to draw a conclusion about _____.	However, evidence about _____ cannot lead to a proper conclusion about _____.

Part A

- You've added parts that explain the meaning of unfamiliar words.

- You've used the words **which is** or **which are** at the beginning of those parts.

- You can often omit those words.

- Here are some examples that use sentences you've worked with:

  > **The duiker, a small African antelope, darted over the hill.**

  > **Kurt had fond memories of the pampas, the grasslands of Argentina.**

  > **Horace was very good with a cant hook, a tool for rolling logs.**

- In some sentences, you may want to keep the words **which is** or **which are.**

- Here's an example:

  > **Leverets, which are young rabbits, must beware of hawks.**

- If you take out the words **which are,** the sentence may be awkward:

  > **Leverets, young rabbits, must beware of hawks.**

Part B

For each item, use a dictionary and rewrite the sentence so it explains what the uncommon word means. The sentence **cannot** use the words **which is** or **which are.**

1. The queen lost a frisette.

2. His samisen was very old.

3. Brian bought and sold suint.

Follow the outline diagram to write about the problems with the directions.

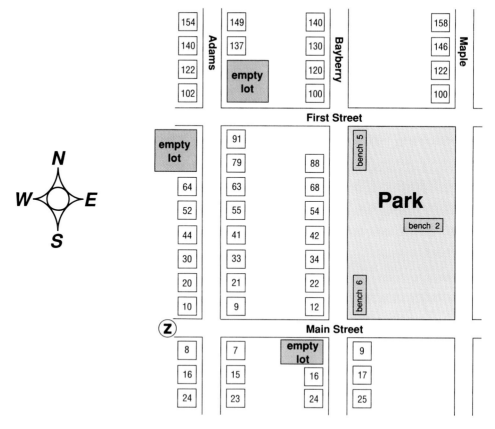

Directions A: Go east on Main.
Turn north by the park.
Go past First Street to the second house on the left.

Directions B: Go east to Adams.
Turn north and go to the third house.

Outline diagram

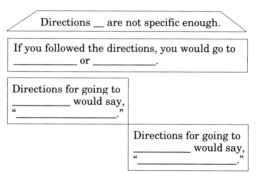

Directions __ are not specific enough.

If you followed the directions, you would go to _____ or _____.

Directions for going to _____ would say,
" _____."

Directions for going to _____ would say,
" _____."

Part D Write the word that completes each sentence with the correct adjective or adverb.

1. a. They are _____ .
   b. They are walking _____ .

   slow

2. a. Alice was _____ .
   b. Alice waited _____ .

   eager

3. a. The bell is ringing _____ .
   b. The bell is _____ .

   loud

4. a. The lions were _____ .
   b. The lions watched _____ .

   patient

5. a. She sings _____ .
   b. Her singing is _____ .

   beautiful

Part E

• Some things in a passage are contradicted by the facts that you know.

• Here's a passage:

   In the land of Mot, everything is exactly the same as it is here except for one thing: people are much larger. The newborn baby is 7 feet tall. The full-grown female is 15 feet tall. The full-grown male is 17 feet tall. Aside from the size of the people, everything else is the same.

Follow the outline diagram to write about the contradiction.

Passage

   I recently learned about a very strange place, the land of Jop. The land of Jop has cities that are like ours. They have the same skyscrapers, the same busy streets, parking garages, department stores, freeways, houses and neighborhoods; the only thing that is different in the land of Jop is the cars. All cars are at least 15 feet wide. According to my sources, everything else in the land of Jop is the same as it is here.

Outline diagram

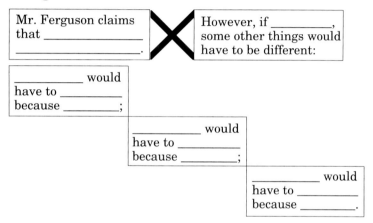

Mr. Ferguson claims that _____ _____.

However, if _____, some other things would have to be different:

_____ would have to _____ because _____;

_____ would have to _____ because _____;

_____ would have to _____ because _____.

Independent Work

Copy the last word in each sentence. Show the part part of speech: AV for adverb; A for adjective; N for noun; P for pronoun.

1. We joined the others.

2. They joked with us.

3. The hike was enjoyable.

4. We went up the new trail.

5. We went far.

6. On Friday, we came back.

7. Jan tripped and sprained her back.

8. When we got home, we were exhausted.

9. Carol thought the trip was boring.

10. Next time, we won't invite her.

Part H Follow the outline diagram to write about the problems with these arguments.

Argument 1: The president of the company made a very bad decision last week. He's going to make another important decision this week. That decision will certainly be stupid.

Argument 2: The argument was ridiculous. It also contained lots of big words. Therefore, big words are ridiculous.

Argument 3: Mr. Jackson's class has a very poor attendance record. Oliver is in Mr. Jackson's class. Oliver must be absent a lot.

Outline diagram

Argument __ uses evidence about _____ to draw a conclusion about _____.

However, evidence about _____ cannot lead to a proper conclusion about _____.

Lesson 45

Part A | Rewrite each incorrect sentence. Use the correct adverb.

1. The traffic moved slow.
2. She talked constantly.
3. He sat quiet.
4. She shouted loudly.
5. They spoke soft.
6. She worked quick.
7. He spoke poorly.
8. She answered correctly.
9. She gave generously.
10. She wrote neat.

Part B | For each item, use a dictionary and rewrite the sentence so it explains what the uncommon word means. The sentence **cannot** use the words **which is** or **which are.**

1. My epergne holds fruit.
2. Kweilin is very attractive.
3. Each soldier had a bandoleer.

Passage A

People seem to leave litter behind wherever they go, even in space. Ever since 1958, when the space age began, missions from Russia, the United States, Japan and several other countries have left tons of space junk in orbit around the earth. Thousands of pieces of old rockets and satellites drift over our heads. Most eventually burn up when they enter the atmosphere.

There's so much of this junk in space today that spaceships must constantly watch for it. In fact, they sometimes have to change course to avoid collisions with space garbage. Such collisions could be deadly, so space agencies devote a lot of effort to preventing them.

Radar and telescopes all over the world follow the positions of thousands of pieces of junk, many no bigger than a marble. Huge computers keep track of this junk. Astronauts and scientists on the ground work together to steer spacecraft safely around the junk. The process is so complicated and expensive that it makes a person wonder: When will people learn to clean up after themselves? Just last June 23, a shuttle from the United States had to change course to avoid some space junk.

Passage B

On Wednesday, June 23, a space shuttle from the United States had to change course to steer clear of some space junk that was drifting around the earth.

Such events are not unusual according to space-agency scientists. Thousands of pieces of junk are in space. A shuttle may have four or five close encounters with space junk on a normal mission.

On Wednesday, the shuttle's course brought it less than a mile from an abandoned Soviet rocket. A collision could have destroyed the shuttle. Astronauts changed the shuttle's course by delaying a rocket firing. They kept to a distance of more than six miles from the Soviet rocket.

Navigators say they are used to keeping a close watch on space junk, but they don't often have to steer around it. Records show that shuttles must change course to steer around space junk only once or twice a year.

Part C continued

Some of the questions below ask where you found the answer. Use this key:

- Write **A** if the answer is found in passage A.
- Write **B** if the answer is found in passage B.
- Write **AB** if the answer is found in both passage A and passage B.

1. When did the space age begin?
2. Where would somebody find the answer to question 1?

3. Name some countries with space programs.
4. Where would somebody find the answer to item 3?

5. How many times a year do spacecraft have to change course to avoid collisions with space junk?
6. Where would somebody find the answer to question 5?

7. After a while, what happens to most space junk?
8. Where would somebody find the answer to question 7?

9. Which country sent up a shuttle that had to change course on June 23?
10. Where would somebody find the answer to question 9?

Follow the outline diagram and write a paragraph that tells about the problem.

Directions: Make an **X** that is one inch high. Make a vertical line that connects the lines on the left side of the **X**.

A.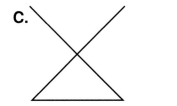

B.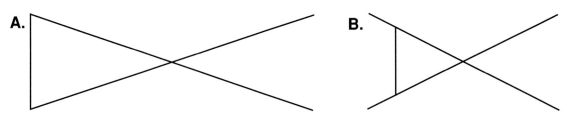

C.

D.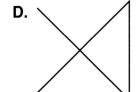

E.

F.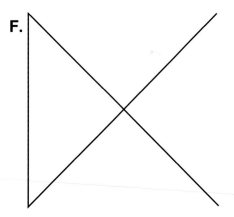

G.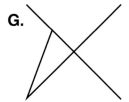

H.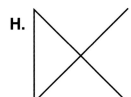

Outline diagram

The directions are not specific enough.

If you followed the directions, you could make figures ____, ____, ____ and ____.

Clear directions for making figure A would say, "_____," and "_____."

Follow the outline diagram to write answers to the following questions. Indicate your source.

Source: ***Farmer's Almanac***
A lunar month is exactly 29.531 days.

Source: ***Hambone Atlas***
Bolivia is a country on the South American continent.

Source: ***Internal Revenue Service***
William Gleason earned $33,770 in 1989
                           $36,400 in 1990
                           $38,790 in 1991
                           $30,001 in 1992

Source: ***Bird Watchers West***
Penguins are found as far south as Bolivia.

Source: ***Mr. William Gleason's Gardener***
• William has lots of money, but he is very cheap.
• I think that a lunar month is about 61 days.
• Bolivia is somewhere south of here.

1. How long is a lunar month?

2. On which continent is the country of Bolivia?

3. How much money did William Gleason earn in 1990?

Outline diagram

According to _____,
_____
_____.

Part F | Follow the outline diagram to describe how monkeys differ from birds.

Table F9

Some Ways That Monkeys Differ From Birds	
monkeys	**birds**
are born alive	hatch from eggs
have lips	have bills
have hair	have feathers

Outline diagram

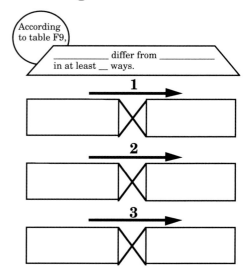

According to table F9, _____ differ from _____ in at least __ ways.

1

2

3

Part G | Copy each sentence and indicate the part of speech for each word.

1. My mother had received many flowers.
2. The smallest dog was tired.
3. They were eating early.
4. I called your brother.

Part A Follow the outline diagram and write a paragraph that tells about the problem.

Directions: Make an **X.**
Connect the ends of the diagonal lines with four straight lines.

A. ◄— 2 inches —►

2 inches

B.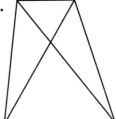

C.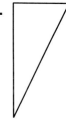

D.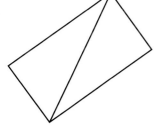

E.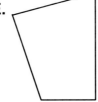

F.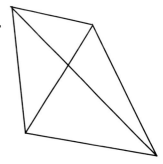

G. ◄—1 inch—►

1 inch

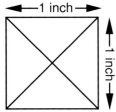

Outline diagram

The directions are not specific enough.

If you followed the directions, you could make figures ____, ____, ____ and ____.

Clear directions for making figure A would say, "_____."

| Rewrite each incorrect sentence. Then label the parts of speech.

1. They were talking soft.
2. The workers would finish quickly.
3. They were rewarded handsome.
4. That truck could stop suddenly.
5. John skates reckless.
6. That clown can fall awkwardly.
7. She speaks nervous.

Part C | Write **Part C** in the left margin of your paper. Then number it from 1 to 12. Read the passages below. Then write the answers to the questions.

Passage A. You may know several kinds of rice, but you may be surprised to know that there are over 5,000 kinds of rice. It comes in long, short and round grains. It may be brown, white, yellow, black—even red or blue. It is grown and eaten on every continent except Antarctica, and it is one of the oldest and most nutritious foods.

Some forms of rice are more nutritious than others. Most rice is milled before it is sold. The milling makes it cook faster and look nicer. Milling removes the bran skin from the shiny grain inside the husk, but it also removes some vitamins, protein and minerals. Brown rice has only the husk removed; the bran skin is left for better nutrition.

Rice is usually cooked whole, in water, steam or broth, until the grain is soft and chewy. Sometimes, rice is ground into flour for bread and puddings.

Many cooks don't know that the amount of water given in a recipe for rice is only an estimate. The reason is that some rice absorbs water much faster than others.

Passage B. There are over 5,000 kinds of rice. It can be brown, white, yellow, black, even red or blue. It can be short, long or round. The earliest evidence of rice cultivation comes from India around 3,000 B.C., making rice one of the oldest known foods.

Most rice is milled before it is sold, to make it cook faster and look nicer. Milling removes the bran skin from the shiny grain inside the husk. Rice with the bran skin left in place is sold as brown rice. Wild rice is not really rice at all, but a water grass that grows only in the swamps and coastal waters of North America.

Rice will double or triple in size during cooking, so one cup of raw rice will yield two and one-half to three cups of cooked rice. The size of servings depends very much on individual taste and local custom, but about one cup of cooked rice is a good portion for one person.

Some of the questions below ask where you found the answer. Use this key:

- Write **A** if the answer is found in passage A.
- Write **B** if the answer is found in passage B.
- Write **AB** if the answer is found in both passage A and passage B.

1. What is removed when brown rice is milled?
2. Which of the sources answers question 1?

3. What is milling?
4. Which of the sources answers question 3?

5. What is wild rice?
6. Which of the sources answers question 5?

7. Why is brown rice more nutritious than milled rice?
8. Which of the sources answers question 7?

9. Is rice grown on every continent?
10. Which of the sources answers question 9?

11. What's a good size for a single serving of rice?
12. Which of the sources answers question 11?

Part D | Follow the outline diagram to write a paragraph that explains the contradiction in these accounts.

Here's the account in the travel book:

The island of Ion is two miles off the coast of Greece. Tour boats leave the dock and go to the island every hour. The trip out to the island is beautiful and takes about 15 minutes. By looking into the green waters, tourists can see a variety of sea creatures, including sharks, porpoises and turtles. The boats pass brave swimmers who are on their way to the island. The island of Ion has five beaches for swimming and snorkeling. Tourists can swim with colorful tropical fish in shallow water.

Here's the guide's account:

You must see Ion. It has five wonderful beaches. It has more colorful fish than you have ever seen in your life. The water is warm and clear. You can see way down. And it is so easy to get to Ion. If you are a good swimmer, you can swim from the coast to Ion in about four minutes.

Outline diagram

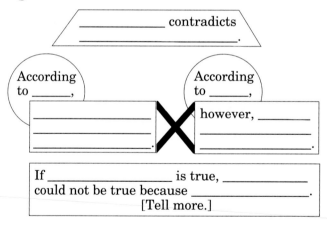

Independent Work

Part E Follow the outline diagram to write answers to the following questions. Indicate your source.

Source: **Mr. Thompson**

"I believe that a centigram is about the weight of a small dog."

Source: **Geology of the World**

The tallest active volcano is Guallatiri, which is in Chile. This volcano last erupted in 1987. It is 19,882 feet tall.

Source: **The Rancher's Almanac**

The shortest day of the year is December 21. The longest day of the year is June 21.

Source: **Jane Doe**

"The tallest active volcano is still erupting somewhere."

Source: **International Table of Weights and Measures**

10 milligrams are 1 centigram; 10 centigrams are 1 decigram.

Source: **Sidney Grump**

"The shortest day of the year occurs around Christmas. It may even be on Christmas."

---

1. When did the world's tallest active volcano last erupt?
2. What is the relationship between a centigram and a decigram?
3. What is the date of the shortest day of the year?

Outline diagram

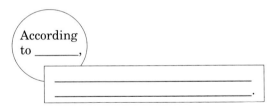

Rewrite these sentences so they tell the meaning of the unfamiliar word. Use a dictionary.

1. For eight years, Ms. Franklin studied glyptography.

2. We love baklava.

3. After answering many ads, Dennis finally found a sinecure.

Lesson 47

Part A

Vocabulary Box	vacuum ocean environment
	diamonds creatures

Part B

- Some words can be more than one part of speech.
- The word **running** is a verb in this sentence:
  The water was running.
- The word **running** is an adjective in this sentence:
  Running water filled our basement.
- The word **running** is a noun in this sentence:
  Running is a very good exercise.
- Some words can be either an adverb or an adjective.
- Here's the word **fast** in two sentences:
  The boys ran fast.
  The boys are fast.

Part C

Copy the last two words of each sentence. Write the part of speech for each of those words.

1. The birds flew high.
2. They worked hard.
3. The problem is hard.
4. The rope held fast.
5. That cloud is high.

6. The game was close.
7. George is fast.
8. The girls sat together.
9. The puppies huddled close.

Write **Part D** in the left margin of your paper. Then number it from 1 to 10. Read the passages below. Then write the answers to the questions.

Passage A. Buck was neither a house dog nor a kennel dog. The whole world was his. He swam or went hunting with the Judge's sons. He kept the Judge's daughters company on long evening walks. On winter nights, he lay at the Judge's feet before the roaring library fire. He carried the Judge's grandsons on his back, or rolled them in the grass, and guarded their footsteps on wild adventures down to the end of the yard. Among the kennel dogs, he walked without fear because he weighed a full 140 pounds. He utterly ignored the house dogs because he was king—king over all living things of Judge Miller's place, humans included.

Passage B. Buck's father, Elmo, was a huge St. Bernard. Elmo had been the Judge's constant companion, and Buck was doing well to follow in the ways of his father. He was not so large. He weighed only 140 pounds. Nevertheless, 140 pounds enabled him to carry himself in royal fashion. During his four years, he had lived the life of a king. He had a pride in himself and was just a little self-centered. But he had not become a spoiled house dog. Hunting and other outdoor delights had kept down the fat and hardened his muscles, and his love of water had kept him in good health.

Some of the questions below ask where you found the answer. Use this key:

- Write **A** if the answer is found in passage A.
- Write **B** if the answer is found in passage B.
- Write **AB** if the answer is found in both passage A and passage B.

1. How much did Buck weigh?
2. Which of the sources answers question 1?
3. How did Buck keep from getting spoiled?
4. Which of the sources answers question 3?
5. What was the name of Buck's father?
6. Which of the sources answers question 5?
7. How did Buck treat the house dogs?
8. Which of the sources answers question 7?
9. Did Buck feel more like a servant or a king?
10. Which of the sources answers question 9?

Follow the outline diagram to explain the inconsistencies in Table F14.

Table F14
Collections from Visuals Plus, Inc.

Collection	Stamps	Medallions	Cards	Posters	Price
Rolling Stones	50	5	10	1	$14
Layers of Wonder	0	0	20	5	$14
Rock Around	10	0	5	3	$8
Gem Stones	0	5	5	5	$20

Outline diagram

_____ is not consistent with _____.

If _____ was consistent with _____, it would cost _____:

_____ would cost _____;
_____ would cost _____;
and _____ would cost _____.

However, [tell about inconsistent collection] _____.

Part F | Follow the outline diagram and write a paragraph that tells about the problem.

Directions: Make a circle that is one inch wide.
Divide the circle into four equal parts by drawing two lines that go from the edge through the center of the circle.

A.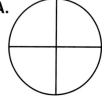

B.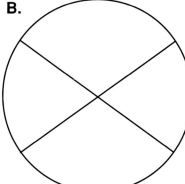

C.

D.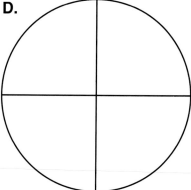

Outline diagram

The directions are not specific enough.

If you followed the directions, you could make figures _____.

Clear directions for making figure __ would say, "_____."

Clear directions for making figure __ would say, "_____."

For each item, use **who, that** or **which** to write the combined sentence. Punctuate the sentences correctly.

1. *This part is essential:*
   The winter solstice occurs in December.
   This part is not essential:
   The winter solstice is the shortest day of the year.

2. *This part is essential:*
   Mercury is more dense than iron, or even gold.
   This part is not essential:
   Mercury is a liquid at room temperature.

3. *This part is essential:*
   They didn't want to go with the Lees.
   This part is not essential:
   The Lees argued constantly.

4. *This part is essential:*
   The argument contained inaccuracies.
   This part is essential:
   The argument was presented by Fran Green.

Part A

- You can make some sentences very parallel.

- Here's a sentence:

  We can buy it in red or yellow.

- Here's a more parallel version of that sentence:

  We can buy it in red or in yellow.

- Here's an even more parallel version:

  We can buy it in red or buy it in yellow.

- Here's a version that is so parallel it becomes two sentences:

  We can buy it in red, or we can buy it in yellow.

- For different purposes you would write different sentences. The original sentence is clear enough for most purposes. If you want to be very clear about what the choice is, you could use the last sentence.

Part B | For each sentence, write two sentences that are more parallel than the sentence shown.

1. That bird sings at sunrise and sunset.

2. We can use dirt from the hill or the river.

3. We will build the house in March or April.

4. Water leaks from the ceiling and the window.

Part C | For each item, replace the word **something** with a better category word. Don't change the rest of the sentence.

1. The wadi, something that is open and usually dry, extended from the foothills to the plains.

2. She purchased cotton cambric, something with a fine weave.

3. They displayed their garnet, something that was brilliant red and clear.

4. I saw a balalaika, something with a triangular shape, a neck, and three strings.

Part D | Follow the outline diagram to write a paragraph that explains the contradiction in the passage and Graph F3.

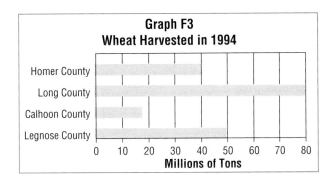

Graph F3
Wheat Harvested in 1994

Passage

    The four counties of Homer, Long, Calhoon and Legnose sold nearly all of their 1994 wheat crop. The four counties harvested about 188 million tons. Long County harvested the most and Calhoon the least. Homer County sold all that it harvested—40 tons. The other counties sold between 80% and 95% of the amount they harvested. Calhoon County had the smallest percentage. It sold 20 million tons, which was only 80% of its harvest. Long County sold 75 million tons, which was more than 90% of its harvest.

Outline diagram

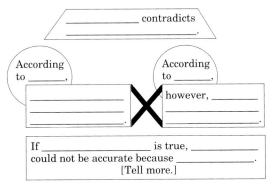

Part E

For each item, use **who, that** or **which** to write the combined sentence. Punctuate the sentences correctly.

1. *This part is essential:*
   She ordered the seat covers in puce.
   This part is not essential:
   Puce is a dark purple.

2. *This part is essential:*
   Our neighbors helped us install the antenna.
   This part is essential:
   Those neighbors live to the east.

3. *This part is essential:*
   Tim had a picture of a pterodactyl.
   This part is essential:
   That pterodactyl was flying over a swamp.

4. *This part is essential:*
   We had studied pterodactyls.
   This part is not essential:
   Pterodactyls were prehistoric flying reptiles.

Follow the outline diagram to write answers to the following questions. Indicate your source.

Source: **Citizen's Almanac**

The most powerful earthquake ever recorded occurred in Japan in 1933. The earthquake had a reading of 8.9 on the Richter scale.

Source: **Dennis Atlas**

The largest lake that borders the U.S. is Lake Superior, which is 81,000 square miles. The largest lake that is totally inside the U.S. is Lake Michigan, which is 67,900 square miles.

Source: **Official Book of Presidents**

Calvin Coolidge was president from 1923 to 1929.
Herbert Hoover was president from 1929 to 1933.

Source: **Precipitation Yearly**

In 1950, Florida had 39 inches of rainfall in a 24-hour period. This was the largest amount of rain ever recorded in one 24-hour period.

---

1. In what year did the largest amount of rainfall in a 24-hour period?

2. What was the Richter-scale reading for the most powerful earthquake in the twentieth century?

3. What's the name and size of the largest lake that is totally inside the U.S.?

4. Who was President of the United States in 1926?

Outline diagram

Lesson 49

Part A | Rewrite each sentence, using a general category word to replace **something.**

1. The city was overrun with cholera, something that is serious and often fatal.

2. We watched a felucca, something that moves gracefully on the water.

3. Their house looked good with the new pantile, something that is curved so it overlaps.

Part B

- You've learned that you need a comma to show a part that is added but is not necessary.

- That rule holds if you add a whole sentence. Those combined sentences have a joining word: **and, but, or.**

- Here are some examples:

    This sentence is first, and this sentence is second.

    This sentence could be first, or this sentence could be first.

    This sentence could be second, but this sentence is second.

- The added part of each sentence is underlined. Each added part is a complete sentence. That's why there's a comma before that part.

- Here are sentences that do not have a complete sentence after the joining word. These sentences do not need a comma:

    This sentence is complete and punctuated correctly.

    This sentence is complete but short.

    This sentence may be a little longer or a lot longer.

- The part after the joining word is not a complete sentence; therefore, no comma is needed.

Rewrite each sentence so it is two perfectly parallel sentences joined together.

1. She was small but very strong.

2. Marsha will go shopping or swimming.

3. That dog sleeps and barks.

4. My uncle will visit on Monday or Tuesday.

For each item, write inconsistent or contradictory.

1. Emily is eight years old. She received three presents for her tenth birthday.

2. He wore dirty clothes and worked in a very poor neighborhood. He was one of the richest men in the entire city.

3. She is extremely wealthy. I saw her in a baby carriage last week.

4. It was a bright morning and Scott walked west across the open field. His shadow was behind him.

Vocabulary Box

carnivore   herbivore

predator   survive

Part F | Follow the outline diagram and write a paragraph that tells about the problem.

    Directions: Make a line that is one inch long and make a half circle.

                    Place the half circle so its ends touch the ends of the line.

A.    **B.**   **C.**    **D.**

Outline diagram

> The dirctions are not specific enough.

> If you followed the directions, you could make figures _____.

> Clear directions for drawing figure A would say, "_____."

Part G | Copy each sentence. Indicate the part of speech for each word.

1. Our old car runs well.

2. The latest newspaper had 20 pages.

3. The new outfit is handsome.

4. They followed us closely.

Lesson 50 – Test 5

Follow the outline diagram to write a paragraph describing the contradictions between the account and the table.

Table F15

School	Students	Girls	Boys
Jefferson	555	290	265
Nichols	114	71	43
Thurston	812	408	404
Franklin	680	356	324
Jackson	106	0	106

Account

The school with the largest number of students is Thurston. It has the same number of boys and girls. In three of the other schools, there are more girls than boys. Jackson is a boys' school, so it has no girls. The smallest school is Nichols. It has only 114 students. The school with the largest number of girls is Franklin. Franklin has 356 girls.

Outline diagram

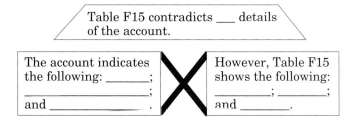

Table F15 contradicts ___ details of the account.

The account indicates the following: _____; _____; and _____ .

However, Table F15 shows the following: _____; _____; and _____.

Part B | Copy the last word of each sentence. Write the letter or letters to show the part of speech.

1. They ran fast.
2. The car moved quickly.
3. My dad is handsome.
4. Our dinners were ready.

5. My cat sleeps frequently.
6. Her work was careful.
7. My aunt visits us often.

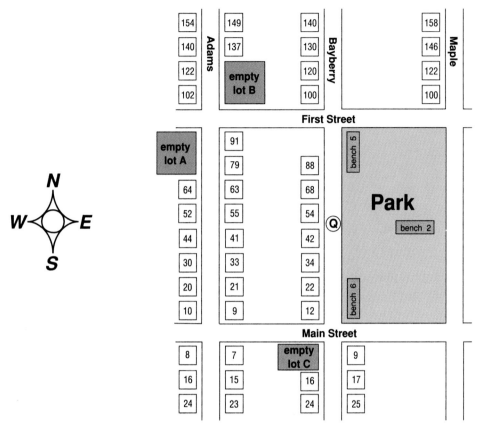

These directions are supposed to tell how to go from the starting point at Q to empty lot A.

Directions: Go north from the starting point at Q.
Turn left at First Street.
Go to the empty lot on the corner of First Street and Adams.

Outline diagram

The directions are not specific enough.

If you followed the directions, you would go ___ _____.

Directions for going to _____ would say, " _____."

Directions for going to _____ would say, " _____."

Rewrite each sentence so the meaning of the unfamiliar word is clear. Use a dictionary.

1. She took three pictures of a handsome ibex.

2. He returned with several tons of mool.

Lesson 51

Part A

> **Sample Items**
>
> A. A drawer is like a pocket.
>
> B. Kites are like eagles.

For each item, write a sentence that is true for both things named.

1. The sun is like a furnace.
2. A cup is like a lake.
3. Snow is like a blanket.
4. Snow is like a polar bear.

Part B | Follow the outline diagram to write about the contradiction.

Here's another claim by Mr. Ferguson:

I recently learned about the land of Nop, which is almost like our country. It has the same type of cities, the same busy streets, the same neighborhoods, freeways and houses. The supermarkets are identical to ours. So are all the shops and stores. Only one thing is different in the land of Nop: Every family has an adult elephant for a pet.

Outline diagram

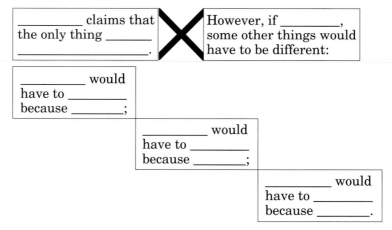

- The verb must agree with the noun or pronoun in the subject of a sentence. If the noun or pronoun tells about **more than one,** the verb must tell about **more than one.** If the noun or the pronoun tells about **one,** the verb must tell about **one.**

- Here's a sentence:

  The flea were brown.

- That's wrong. There's only **one flea,** so the verb must refer to **one.**

- Here's the correct sentence:

  The flea was brown.

- These sentences are correct:

  The biggest flea was brown.
  The dogs' flea was brown.

Part D | For each item, write **was** or **were.**

1. My uncle's car _____ new.
2. The dog's fleas _____ hungry.
3. Jack's eye _____ sore.
4. The campers' pledges _____ important.
5. Our house's chimneys _____ filthy.
6. The farmer's cow _____ old.
7. The girls' cooking _____ bad.

Part E | Rewrite each sentence, using a more specific category word.

1. The bard, someone who also played a harp, entertained us.
2. We saw an osprey, something that feeds on fish.
3. The bears were watching a parr, something with dark crossbars on its sides.

Part F | Rewrite each sentence so it is two perfectly parallel sentences joined together.

1. Their car was wet and muddy.
2. Her cough was painful and persistent.
3. They sang energetically but poorly.

Independent Work

Part G | Copy the last word in each sentence. Write the part of speech.

1. The building was tall.
2. Their relatives lived in the city.
3. That organization buys scrap metal.
4. Mr. Dennis slept often.
5. The elevator went down.
6. The well was deep.
7. She sang loudly.
8. Our dog has a new collar.
9. The village grew daily.
10. Our office was ugly.

For each item, write two sentences—one for each picture. Use both parts in each sentence.

1. Here's a part: The girl has five sisters.
   Here's another part: The girl wore a black coat.

2. Here's a part: Mr. Taylor cleaned the chimney.
   Here's another part: That chimney is near the garage.

3. Here's a part: Lou bought a used car.
   Here's another part: The car had a new engine.

Lesson 52

Part A | Copy each sentence and complete it by adding words that tell what is different about the unfamiliar word.

1. They had a pet mongoose, a carnivorous animal.
2. We wrote palindromes, which are words.
3. He had pictures of a serval, a cat.

Part B | For each item, write **is** or **are.**

1. The tractors' wheels _____ red.
2. The student's pens _____ expensive.
3. The manager's argument _____ ridiculous.
4. The Smith Building's doors _____ unlocked.
5. The building's windows _____ dirty.
6. The children's dog _____ sick.
7. Our mother's cupcakes _____ delicious.
8. Sally's horses _____ fast.

Part C | For each item, write a sentence that is true for each thing named.

1. Her cheeks were like apples.
2. The children's minds were like vacuum cleaners.
3. Each word she spoke was like a drop of honey.

| **Follow the outline diagram to write about the contradiction.**

Here's another claim by Mr. Ferguson:

I recently learned about the land of Hop, which is exactly like our land except that people have only one eye, which is just above their nose. Everything else is the same as it is here.

Outline diagram

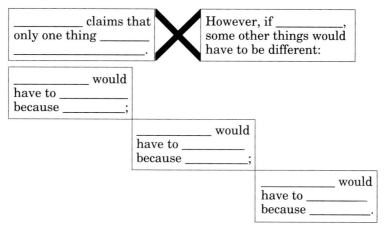

_____ claims that only one thing _____ _____.

However, if _____, some other things would have to be different:

_____ would have to _____ because _____;

_____ would have to _____ because _____;

_____ would have to _____ because _____.

Write the last word for each sentence and indicate the part of speech for the word you wrote.

1. Those motors run _____ .

   | smooth |
   | smoothly |

2. Tom's brother is _____ .

   | strange |
   | strangely |

3. That dog is _____ .

   | clumsy |
   | clumsily |

4. She worked _____ .

   | steady |
   | steadily |

5. His car is _____ .

   | new |
   | newly |

6. Our dog barks _____ .

   | loud |
   | loudly |

7. The carrot is _____ .

   | tasty |
   | tastily |

Part F | Rewrite each sentence so it has two parts that are perfectly parallel. Punctuate the sentence correctly.

1. We will go swimming or hiking.
2. Her dog is small but mean.
3. I bought groceries and flowers.

Part G | Write three or four words that are **palindromes.**

Lesson 53

> **Sample Sentence**
>
> The girls' sunburn _____ painful.

Rewrite each sentence so it has the word of and uses the correct verb, was or were.

1. The campers' spirit _____ high.
2. The door's sides _____ worn.
3. The trains' noise _____ loud.
4. The train's noises _____ irritating.
5. The smokestacks' odor _____ terrible.

Part B | Follow the outline diagram to write about the contradiction.

Here's what Jenny said to her parents:

If our family had a dog, only one thing would change: We would have a nice pet. Everything else would be exactly the same as it is now. We wouldn't even have to buy dog food because the dog could eat leftovers.

Outline diagram

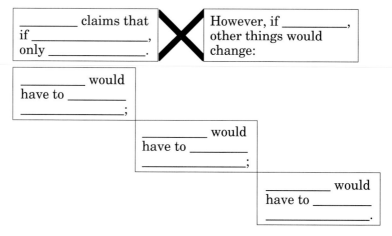

- You've learned that if a sentence has an action verb, the last word in the sentence is not an adjective, but an adverb. If the sentence has an **is** verb, the last word is an adjective.

- There are other verbs that require adjectives. These are called **verbs of the senses. Verbs of the senses** describe the way you sense things. You **touch** them, **smell** them, **hear** them, **taste** them, **feel** them or **imagine** them.

- All verbs that refer to the senses use adjectives.

- All these sentences are correct:

> **That room** smells terrible.   [**not terribly**]
>
> **That lettuce** tastes sour.   [**not sourly**]
>
> **I** feel wonderful.   [**not wonderfully**]

Part D | All these sentences end in an adjective. Write **S** if the verb is a verb of the senses or **X** if it is not. Rewrite each sentence that you mark with an **X** so it ends with an adverb.

1. Those roses smell fragrant.
2. The dog barked loud.
3. The dog sounded loud.
4. Her coat felt rough.
5. Her coat protected thorough.

6. Her coat looked smooth.
7. She spoke smooth.
8. Her words sounded smooth.
9. She ran smooth.

Part E | Follow the outline diagram to explain parallel features that are opposite.

- Summer is like life.

- _____ is like death.

Outline diagram

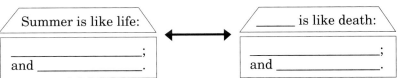

Part F | Follow the outline diagram to write about the problem with the directions.

Directions: Make a star that is 2 inches across.

A.

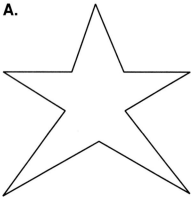

B.

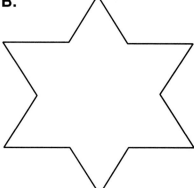

C.

D.

Outline diagram

The directions are not specific enough.

If you followed the directions, you could make figures _____.

Clear directions for drawing figure A would say, "_____."

| Copy each sentence and write the part of speech for each word.

1. She had one complaint.
2. Our other dog barks constantly.
3. Her paintings were colorful.
4. She painted dogs occasionally.

Lesson 54

Part A

Vocabulary Box	Utah Promontory Pacific
	opposite Union

Part B   Write **S** if the verb is a verb of the senses or **X** if it is not. Rewrite each sentence that you mark with an **X** so it ends with an adverb.

1. She spoke sweet.
2. She looked sweet.
3. The melon tastes sweet.
4. Our car runs quiet.
5. Our car sounds quiet.
6. Our car feels rough.
7. The TV sounds loud.
8. The announcer spoke loud.
9. Our dog smells clean.

Part C   Rewrite each sentence so it has the word **of** and uses the correct verb, **is** or **are.**

1. The group's decisions _____ surprising.
2. A dogs' disease _____ developing.
3. Bob's efforts _____weak.
4. The girls' concentration _____ amazing.
5. Our students' math performance _____ good.

Follow the outline diagram to write about the contradiction.

Here's another report by Mr. Ferguson:

    I have learned that there is a strange land called Zop. In that land, everything is exactly as it is here except for one thing: Everybody has three arms and three hands. The third arm is in the middle of the back. That arm usually has a right hand, but sometimes it has a left hand. Aside from this feature, everything in Zop is the same as it is here.

Outline diagram

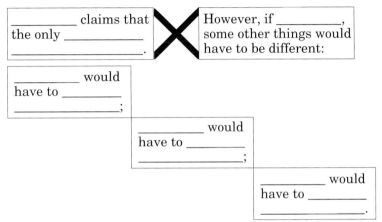

Independent Work

Rewrite each sentence so it is completely parallel. Punctuate the sentence correctly.

1. She reads fast but accurately.

2. The note was long and confusing.

3. We'll buy a house trailer or a cabin.

Each item has the first part of a description. Write a complete sentence for each item.

1. They went to an amusement park, a place where

   _____ .

2. We learned a lot in geography, the study of

   _____ .

Part G Write two sentences, one for each picture. Use both parts in each sentence.

Here's a part: The large man was a bank robber.

Here's another part: That bank robber was carrying a package.

Part A | Rewrite each sentence so it has the word **of** and uses the correct verb, **was** or **were.**

1. Tom's tones _____ sad.

2. The wheel's spokes _____ filthy.

3. The bands' performance _____ lively.

Part B | Follow the outline diagram to write a paragraph that explains any contradictions in the passages. Then write another paragraph that includes both reasons for the decline of the bluebird.

Passage 1

Bluebirds are disappearing from North America. The reason is the increased population of sparrows and starlings. Starlings are not native to North America. Sparrows and starlings like to nest in the same places that bluebirds like. Bluebirds are mild-mannered, peaceful animals, so the frisky sparrows and starlings find it easy to drive the bluebirds out of their nests and move into the stolen homes.

Passage 2

Bluebirds are disappearing from North America. They have always preferred to nest in old fence posts and rotting trees near farms and on the outskirts of towns. As our cities grow larger, most rotten trees are cut down, and metal fence posts have largely replaced the old wooden kind. The lack of proper nesting places is the only reason for the decline of the population of bluebirds.

Outline diagram

Passage 2 contradicts passage 1.

_____ indicates that _____.

However, _____ indicates that _____.

Two reasons explain the disappearance of bluebirds from North America.

Part C | Complete each sentence by adding words that tell what is different about the unfamiliar word.

1. My uncle saw the Japura, a river.

2. We read about Oeneus, a mythical king.

3. The villagers were afraid of the mamba, a poisonous snake.

Part D | For each item, write a sentence that is true for each thing named.

1. When the children went to the playground, they acted like puppies.

2. The worker's hands were like sheets of sandpaper.

Independent Work

Part E | Rewrite each sentence so it is completely parallel. Punctuate the sentence correctly.

1. We have homework in math and science.

2. Their assignment was short but unclear.

3. They will paint the garage or go to the coast.

Some of the items are unclear. Rewrite those items so they are clear.

1. She buys more at a grocery store than a gas station.
2. She works faster in the morning than her brother.
3. Our dog eats more dry dog food than table scraps.
4. Our dog eats more than our cat.
5. She wanted to do more painting than gymnastics.
6. Sidney painted more than his little brother.
7. Jenny planted more in the garden than the window box.

Each sentence tells about a situation that appears to be impossible. Think of situations in which these things could be possible. Follow the outline diagram to explain the apparent inconsistency.

1. Orville weighed over 200 pounds, but little Hilda could move him and hold him up with one arm.
2. It was midnight, but we could see the sun at the horizon.

Outline diagram

Possibly, _____
_____.

Lesson 56

Part A | Rewrite each sentence so it has the word **of** and uses the correct verb, **was** or **were.**

1. The islands' ruler _____ unfriendly.

2. The crew's bosses _____ tough.

3. The children's mother _____ hurrying home.

Part B | Write **Part B** in the left margin of your paper. Then number it from 1 to 12. Read the passages below. Then write the answers to the questions.

Passage A

Jack London wrote many thrilling stories about wolves, dogs, sea adventures and the gold rush in Alaska. From the beginning, Jack had a strong taste for adventure. As a youth, he was a hobo who rode trains throughout the United States.

When he was 17, he sailed for Japan to hunt seals. The hunting party met with a typhoon at sea, and London wrote a description of the storm that won a writing contest in 1893. It was his first publication.

Later, London finished high school, but he was unsatisfied with university life. In 1896, the first reports of Alaskan gold reached San Francisco, and London chose to begin another adventure. He joined four other men on a steamship bound for Alaska. He spent a year in Alaska, where he got material for his best-known stories, including *The Call of the Wild.*

Passage B

Buck did not read the newspapers, or he would have known that trouble was coming, not just for himself, but for other dogs with strong muscles and warm fur. Men searching in Alaskan darkness had found a yellow metal. Thousands of men were now rushing into the Northland. These men wanted dogs, and the dogs they wanted were heavy animals—dogs strong enough to work—dogs with thick coats to protect them from the cold.

Buck lived at a big house in a sunny California valley. Judge Miller's place, it was called. It stood back from the road, huge and half hidden among the trees. There were long, winding driveways, small houses for servants, green fields and a well.

Buck ruled over this territory. Here he was born, and here he had lived four years of his life.

Some of the questions below ask where you found the answer. Use this key:

- Write **A** if the answer is found in passage A.
- Write **B** if the answer is found in passage B.
- Write **AB** if the answer is found in both passage A and passage B.

1. Where was Jack London going when he encountered a typhoon?

2. Which source answers question 1?

3. Why was trouble coming for Buck and some other dogs?

4. Which source answers question 3?

5. Did Jack London ever finish high school?

6. Which source answers question 5?

7. When did the Alaska gold rush begin?

8. Which source answers question 7?

9. Why doesn't Buck read the newspapers?

10. Which source answers question 9?

11. Who wrote *The Call of the Wild*?

12. Which source answers question 11?

Growing a vegetable garden is like saving money.

- Why do you grow a garden?
- When is a garden a lot of work?
- When are people glad that they have a vegetable garden?
- When would other people envy your vegetable garden?

Outline diagram

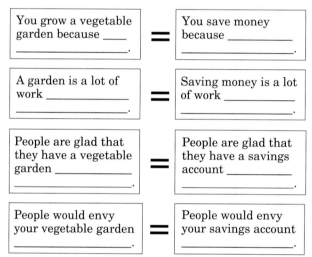

You grow a vegetable garden because ____ _____.	=	You save money because _____ _____.
A garden is a lot of work _____ _____.	=	Saving money is a lot of work _____ _____.
People are glad that they have a vegetable garden _____ _____.	=	People are glad that they have a savings account _____ _____.
People would envy your vegetable garden _____.	=	People would envy your savings account _____.

- Some sentences have more than one noun in the subject. The main noun comes before the words **of, in** or **on.** You use the main noun to figure out if the verb tells about one or more than one.

- Here's a sentence:

    The girl in the pictures was attractive.

- The main noun is **girl.** It comes before **in.** There was one girl. So the verb is **was.**

- Here's another sentence:

    The numbers on the page were large.

- The main noun is **numbers.** It comes before **on.** The word **numbers** tells about more than one. So the verb is **were.**

- Remember, find the main noun. Make the verb show the same number as the main noun.

Sample Sentence

The possessions of the man _____ in a chest.

For each item, write a simpler sentence that has only the main noun and the correct verb, **was** or **were.**

1. The tax on her purchases _____ two dollars.

2. The group of soldiers _____ resting.

3. The flights of our plane _____ exciting.

Part F | Rewrite the sentences that are incorrect.

1. Her effort was impressive.
2. She learned easy.
3. She looked great.
4. She moved graceful.
5. She wandered aimless.
6. Her skin was smooth.
7. Her cooking smelled delicious.
8. Her cooking tasted delicious.

Part G | Follow the outline diagram to write about the contradiction.

Here's another report by Mr. Ferguson:

I have recently learned about the land of Plop. The only difference between that land and ours is that in the land of Plop the largest trees are 10 feet tall. Aside from that difference, everything is the same as it is here.

(**Hint:** Think about the parts of trees and how they are used.)

Outline diagram

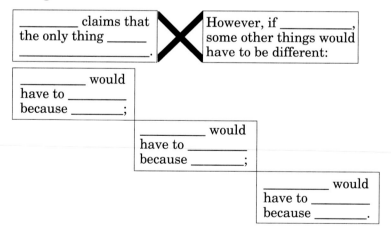

Part A | For each item, write a simpler sentence that has only the main noun and the correct verb, **was** or **were.**

1. The colors of our maple tree _____ brilliant.

2. Parts of our car _____ in the garage.

3. The effort of the workers _____ impressive.

Part B
- You're going to figure out rules.
- You'll describe the rules with sentences that start with **if.**
- Each rule will tell what someone has to do to cause an outcome and what the outcome is.
- Later, you'll describe how to test the rules.

Follow the outline diagram to write a rule about Joe and his girlfriend.

What Joe did   **What his girlfriend did**

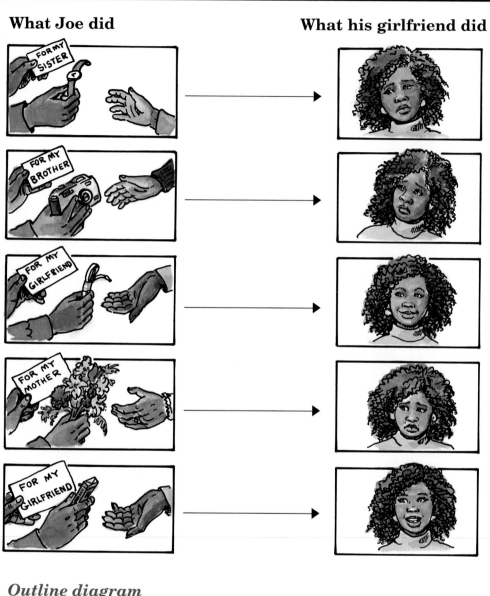

Outline diagram

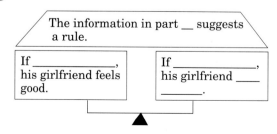

The information in part __ suggests a rule.

If _____, his girlfriend feels good.

If _____, his girlfriend ____ _____.

Follow the outline diagram on page 242 to write a rule about Ms. Taylor.

Tuesday morning

Ms. Taylor

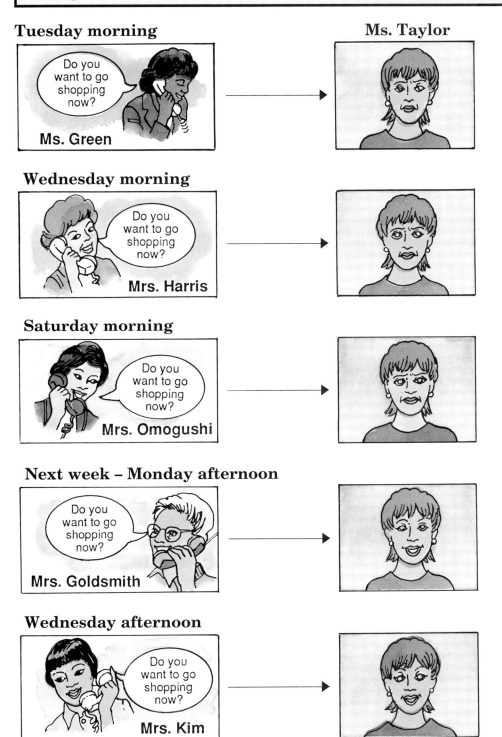

Wednesday morning

Saturday morning

Next week – Monday afternoon

Wednesday afternoon

Outline diagram

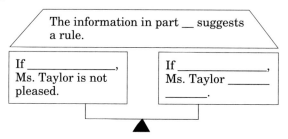

The information in part ___ suggests a rule.

If _____,
Ms. Taylor is not pleased.

If _____,
Ms. Taylor _____
_____.

Part E | Follow the outline diagram and write parallel sentences.

Owning a car is like owning a horse.

Outline diagram

[owning a car] **=** [owning a horse]

Independent Work

Part F | Write each sentence so it is two parallel sentences joined with **and, or** or **but.** Punctuate the sentence properly.

1. The dog was energetic but irritating.
2. Martha had a sore leg and a bruised ankle.
3. My sister will quit her job or go insane.

Rewrite each sentence so it uses **of.**

1. The spider's back was striped.

2. The table's legs had scratches on them.

3. The cars' windshields were dirty.

4. The spiders' nest was hidden.

Write about the problem with Jerry's conclusion.

Here's what Jerry said:

The committee that is planning the school picnic came out with some conclusions and recommendations that are ridiculous. The committee actually wanted to start the picnic at 7:30 in the morning on Saturday. You'll have to admit that's pretty insane.

Eric Volt is on that committee. I used to think that he was a pretty smart guy, but it's obvious that if he's on a committee that comes up with dumb conclusions, he must be pretty dumb.

Outline diagram

However, evidence about _____ cannot lead to _____.

Lesson 58

Part A | Rewrite each sentence so it has only a main noun and a possessive word before the noun. The possessive word will need an apostrophe.

1. The windows of the building were dirty.
2. The title of the book was short.
3. The leaves of the trees were colorful.
4. The leg of our dog was injured.
5. The keys of the typewriter were sticking.
6. The color of the leaves was changing.

Part B | Read the passage. Write the number of each sentence that has a problem and rewrite those problem sentences.

Passage

¹ Six workers remodeled the old Remco Building. ² That group of workers were very busy the first day. ³ The first thing the workers did was to tear out all the inside walls. ⁴ The inside looked strangely without walls. ⁵ On the next day, the workers remove parts of the roof. ⁶ The workers used cutting tools. ⁷ They cut quick. ⁸ Pieces of roofing was all over the place. ⁹ Rain starts falling just before 5 p.m. ¹⁰ The workers worked too slow. ¹¹ Sheets of water flooded the inside. ¹² The first floor looked like a swimming pool. ¹³ The workers start making jokes about the water. ¹⁴ One worker said, "We won't have to take a shower today."

Read the passage and the possibilities. Follow the outline diagram to describe how Joe could test each possibility.

Passage

Joe had a girlfriend who was happy sometimes and unhappy at other times. Joe thought about her moods and figured out this rule: **When I give somebody else a present, she feels bad. When I give her a present, she feels wonderful.**

As Joe thought about this rule and about the evidence that he had to support the rule, he decided that there were other possible rules that could explain the way his girlfriend behaved. Maybe she just happened to like the two things he gave her—shoelaces and gum. Maybe she was just grouchy on the days that he gave somebody else a present.

Joe decided that he would test the rule that he had made up. His test would have to rule out other possibilities.

Other possibilities

1. Joe's girlfriend is unhappy unless the gift she gets is shoelaces or gum.

2. Joe's girlfriend just happened to be happy on days that she received gifts from Joe.

3. Joe's girlfriend would feel sad if anybody gave presents to other people.

Outline diagram

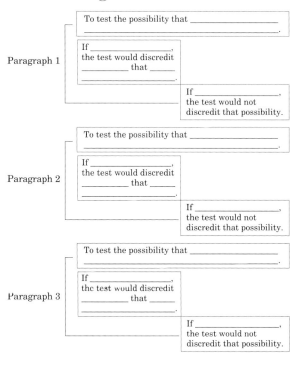

To test the possibility that _____ .

Paragraph 1

If _____, the test would discredit _____ that _____ .

If _____, the test would not discredit that possibility.

To test the possibility that _____ .

Paragraph 2

If _____, the test would discredit _____ that _____ .

If _____, the test would not discredit that possibility.

To test the possibility that _____ .

Paragraph 3

If _____, the test would discredit _____ that _____ .

If _____, the test would not discredit that possibility.

Part D | Follow the outline diagram to write about the problem with the description.

Description: The chair had a high back and a torn seat.

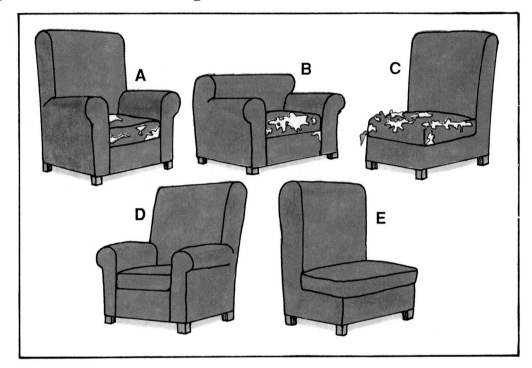

Outline diagram

The description is not _____.

It could tell about _____.

A good description for chair A would say:
_____.

Part E | Write a good description for chair B.
Write a good description for chair E.

Use the word **who, that** or **which** to write combined sentences. Use a comma if it is appropriate.

1. *This part is essential:*
   We washed a car.
   This part is essential:
   The car was covered with mud.

2. *This part is essential:*
   The dinner was cold.
   This part is not essential:
   That dinner was served in the main dining room.

3. *This part is essential:*
   A young woman lost a contact lens.
   This part is not essential:
   That woman had just come into the store.

4. *This part is essential:*
   We listened to my uncle.
   This part is not essential:
   He loves to tell jokes.

5. *This part is essential:*
   I thanked the woman.
   This part is essential:
   That woman found my wallet.

Lesson 59

Part A | Follow the outline diagram and write parallel sentences.

Doing well in school is like climbing a slippery hill.

Outline diagram

| [doing well in school] | = | [climbing a slippery hill] |

Part B | For each item, the missing verb is either **was** or **were**. Rewrite each sentence so it doesn't have the word **of**. One of the words in each sentence will need an apostrophe.

1. The position of the knife _____ dangerous.

2. The wings of the plane _____ damaged.

3. The wheels of her truck _____ shiny.

4. The sound of the motorboats _____ annoying.

5. The curves of the road _____ rough.

Part C Follow the outline diagram to describe how to test each possibility.

Rule

If somebody asks Ms. Taylor to go shopping in the morning, she is not pleased. If somebody asks her to go shopping in the afternoon, she is pleased.

Other possibilities

- Ms. Taylor was in a bad mood one week.
- Ms. Taylor was grumpy because she didn't like some of the women.

Outline diagram

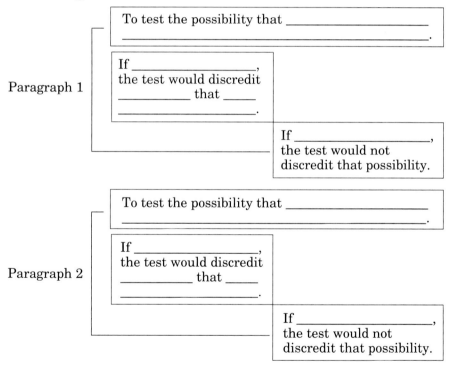

Paragraph 1

To test the possibility that _____ _____.

If _____, the test would discredit _____ that _____ _____.

If _____, the test would not discredit that possibility.

Paragraph 2

To test the possibility that _____ _____.

If _____, the test would discredit _____ that _____ _____.

If _____, the test would not discredit that possibility.

Read the passage. Write the number of each sentence that has a problem and rewrite those problem sentences. The first sentence is correct.

Passage

¹ Fran Edison teaches gymnastics to a group of girls. ² She makes sure that her girls practice regular. ³ The girls come in at 4:00 every day except Saturday and Sunday. ⁴ They practice every day until 6:30, and then they left to go home. ⁵ The best student in Fran's group is little Donna Brown. ⁶ She does difficult tricks easy. ⁷ She works steady. ⁸ She learns quick. ⁹ Next week, Fran will have a meet between her gymnasts and another team.

¹⁰ The other team of girls are from Ocean City. ¹¹ Those girls have won twenty meets in a row. ¹² The last time they lost a meet was two years ago. ¹³ Fran believes that her gymnasts can beat the group from Ocean City. ¹⁴ Fran says, "My girls look polished." ¹⁵ She tells others that her girls are ready and that they will win.

Independent Work

Part E

For each item, write one sentence that is true for both things named. Start with a pronoun that could refer to either thing named.

1. A good education is like money in the bank.

2. The people in the ocean looked like corks.

3. Mr. Wilson's body looks like a pear.

For each item, answer both questions.

1. The wind's direction _____ changing.
   A. Is the verb **was** or **were?**
   B. The direction belonged to _____.

2. The water's colors _____ bright.
   A. Is the verb **was** or **were?**
   B. The colors belonged to _____.

3. The teams' ranking _____ higher than before.
   A. Is the verb **was** or **were?**
   B. The ranking belongs to _____.

4. My cousin's parents _____ old.
   A. Is the verb **was** or **were?**
   B. The parents belong to _____.

5. Their dogs' collars _____ smelly.
   A. Is the verb **was** or **were?**
   B. The collars belong to _____.

Part G

Write a paragraph that describes the problem with Linda's reasoning.

Here's what Linda said:

I can't believe that Kathleen would cheat and lie. But the evidence is clear. Her older sister was caught cheating on a test. Kathleen and her sister are members of the same family, so Kathleen must cheat and lie, too.

Outline diagram

Lesson 60 – Test 6

Part A | For each item, write a complete description. Use a dictionary.

1. They observed a kakapo, something that comes out at night.
2. We considered going in a fiacre, something pulled by horses.
3. She talked to over 100 octogenarians, people.

Part B | Write each sentence with the correct last word.

1. The band played _____.

   | loud |
   | loudly |

2. The flowers smelled _____.

   | fragrant |
   | fragrantly |

3. The sunset looked _____.

   | colorful |
   | colorfully |

4. The dogs howled _____.

   | constant |
   | constantly |

5. The jacket felt _____.

   | warm |
   | warmly |

Rewrite each sentence so it does not have the word **of** but has a possessive word and **was** or **were** for the verb.

1. The car of the robbers _____ in the woods.

2. The peaks of the mountain _____ covered with snow.

3. The hooves of the pig _____ dirty.

Part D

Follow the outline diagram and write at least three pairs of parallel sentences.

Owning a car is like owning a horse.

Outline diagram

[owning a car] = [owning a horse]

Part E

Work each item.

1. An alarm clock is like a rude person.

    Write a sentence that starts with the appropriate pronoun and could describe either an alarm clock or a rude person.

2. An umbrella is like a roof.

    Write a sentence that starts with the appropriate pronoun and could describe either an umbrella or a roof.

Part A

- These sentences name an actor and tell what the actor did:

  Al gave his brother a gift.

  Norma purchased the machine.

  The rain washed gravel from our driveway.

- All those sentences are called **active** because they first name the actor and then tell the action. Al **gave** something; Norma **purchased** something; the rain **did** something.

- The sentences can be changed from active to passive by reversing the order so the actor is not named first:

  His brother **was given a gift by Al.**

  The machine **was purchased by Norma.**

  The gravel from our driveway **was washed away by the rain.**

- These sentences are not great because they have too many words and they are too complicated. Active sentences are better.

Part B | Oral exercise. Name the actor and say the sentence that starts with the actor.

1. The birds were seen by the hunters.
2. The grapes were eaten by the children.
3. The rabbits were fed by Alice.
4. She was handed a book by the teacher.
5. They were awarded a prize by the principal.

These sentences are passive. Rewrite the sentences so they are active.

1. The trees were cut by the loggers.
2. The roots were removed by the tractor.
3. That music was played by a band.
4. Five bananas were eaten by her monkey.
5. Our horses were fed by the workers.

Part D

- Some things cause outcomes. You have figured out ways to test the causes of different outcomes. Something **caused** Joe's girlfriend to act differently at different times.
- You also worked with problems involving strange lands like Jop, Nop, and Hop. Changes in one thing **cause** changes in other things.
- Some arguments are faulty because they present evidence that two events occur around the same time or they occur together. Those arguments then conclude that one event caused the other.
- Here's the rule:

    Evidence about events occurring together does not lead to the conclusion that one event causes the other.

Mr. Jackson went to Detroit, and it snowed in Detroit. Then Mr. Jackson went to New York, and it snowed in New York. Mr. Jackson's trips cause snow.

Outline diagram

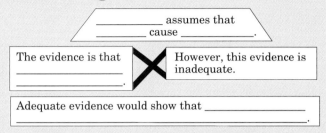

_____ assumes that _____ cause _____.

The evidence is that _____.

However, this evidence is inadequate.

Adequate evidence would show that _____.

**Sample
Response**

The argument assumes that Mr. Jackson's trips cause snow. The evidence is that Mr. Jackson went to two cities and it snowed in those cities. However, this evidence is inadequate. Adequate evidence would show that Mr. Jackson went to 2 cities each month during the year and it snowed in every city.

Follow the outline diagram in the sample above to explain the problems with this argument.

Argument 1: Robins are not around during cold weather. Robins are around during warm weather. The way to make the weather warmer is to keep robins around.

- Sometimes, people write sentences that are supposed to be parallel but aren't. Typically, those sentences list three or more things.
- Here's an example:

  They rode horses, played catch and were tired.
- The verb **were** is not parallel.
- You can fix up the sentence by rewriting it as two sentences:

  They rode horses and played catch. They were tired.
- Sometimes, you can fix up the sentence by making the parts parallel.
- Here's a sentence that doesn't have parallel parts:

  The class had 15 girls, 12 boys, and the teacher was good.
- Here's the rewritten sentence:

  The class had 15 girls, 12 boys and a good teacher.
- Or:

  The class had 15 girls, 12 boys and a teacher who was good.

Part G Rewrite each sentence so the last part is parallel to the other parts.

1. We mowed the yard, raked the grass and were washing the car.
2. We should study hard and have money saved if we want to go to college.
3. She was tall, graceful and had a lot of skill.
4. Our dog is loyal, friendly and obeys well.
5. Her horse was strong, fast and was a beauty.

Part H

- You've worked with arguments about groups and individuals. These arguments make the mistake of drawing conclusions about an individual from evidence about a group, or the mistake of drawing conclusions about a group from evidence about an individual.

- These arguments are called **part-whole arguments.**

- The **individual** is the **part;** the **group** is the **whole.**

- Part-whole arguments can refer to parts that are not individuals and wholes that are not groups. They can refer to any part and any whole.

- Here are the rules:

  ✔ You can't draw a proper conclusion about **a whole** from evidence about **a part;**

  ✔ You can't draw a proper conclusion about **a part** from evidence about **a whole;**

  ✔ You can't draw a proper conclusion about **a part** from evidence about **another part.**

Part I

Identify the part and the whole in each argument. Then follow the outline diagram to explain the problem with argument 1.

Argument 1: The car has the finest heater made. Therefore, the car must be a superior car.

Argument 2: Dr. Brown and Dr. Dennis have offices in the Ferris Building. Dr. Brown's office is very cold every time I'm in it. Therefore, Dr. Dennis's office must also be very cold.

Argument 3: I have seen beautiful banana trees in North Cove on Diller Island. The whole island must be covered with banana trees.

Outline diagram

Argument __ uses evidence about _____ to draw a conclusion about _____.	However, evidence about _____ does not lead to a proper conclusion about _____.

Part J

Follow the outline diagram in Part I to write about the problems with arguments 2 and 3 in Part I.

Part K

Write at least three pairs of parallel sentences. Tell about a dog and then tell about a person.

Owning a dog is like having another person in the family.

Outline diagram

[a dog]	=	[a person]

Lesson 62

Part A

Sample Sentence

They were followed by me.

These sentences are passive. Rewrite them so they are active. Watch the pronouns.

1. They were guarded by me.

2. I was bothered by him.

3. She was admired by them.

4. He was corrected by her.

5. They were entertained by me.

Part B | Follow the outline diagram to explain the problems with the argument.

Andy's argument: Coach Smith is very upset because he lost his lucky pair of green socks. Here's what happened: Our team had been losing a lot of basketball games. Then Coach Smith started wearing his lucky green socks. He wore the green socks, and our team beat Franklin High School. He wore the green socks, and our team beat Lincoln High School. I don't blame the coach for being upset over losing those socks. We're playing Thurston High School tonight, and we probably won't win without those lucky socks.

Outline diagram

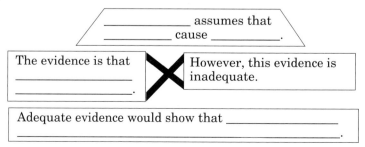

Part C | Rewrite each sentence so the last part is parallel to the other parts.

1. Howard works slowly, carefully and is steady.

2. Their truck had comfortable seats, a large storage area and was powerful.

3. She wore a wool coat, black boots, and her hat was new.

4. The puppies were happy, playful and had a lot of energy.

5. Mrs. Rivera's soup is hot, spicy and has a good taste.

Part D | For each argument, write the name used in the evidence. Indicate whether it is a part or a whole. Then write the name used in the conclusion and indicate whether it is a part or a whole.

Argument 1: The salad we are eating is super. Therefore, the whole dinner will be super.

Argument 2: The front door of the Wilson house squeaks when you open it. The back door must also squeak.

Argument 3: I didn't read the whole book, but I know that it is boring. I read the first chapter, and it was terribly boring.

Argument 4: I would never own a house built by Thompson Construction. The reason is that Thompson Construction builds houses that are inexpensive. I don't mind that part, but I need a good heating system in my house, and an inexpensive house can't have a very good heating system.

Part E | Follow the outline diagram to explain the problem with each argument in Part D.

Outline diagram

| Argument __ uses evidence about _____ to draw a conclusion about _____. | ✕ | However, evidence about _____ does not lead to a proper conclusion about _____. |

Part F | Write the sentences with the word **was** or **were.**

1. The reflection of the trees _____ bright yellow.

2. The exhaust sound of the trucks _____ deafening.

3 The wristbands of the jacket _____ poorly made.

4 The pieces of evidence _____ not very strong.

5. The direction of his arguments _____ always the same.

Part A   Follow the outline diagram to explain the problem with the argument.

Argument

We hired Dr. Gregory to keep dinosaurs out of our city parks, and Dr. Gregory is doing a marvelous job. By placing his little statues of sharks in parks, he is able to scare off dinosaurs. We visited all of our parks last week, and I am happy to announce that we did not see a single dinosaur. Furthermore, we didn't even see signs that dinosaurs had been around. Congratulations to Dr. Gregory, and boo to his critics who say that he does not deserve the high salary our city is paying him.

Outline diagram

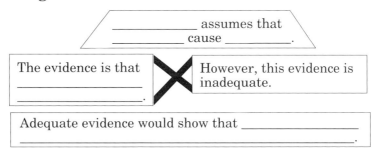

_____ assumes that _____ cause _____.

The evidence is that _____ _____.

However, this evidence is inadequate.

Adequate evidence would show that _____ _____.

Part B

- You've fixed up sentences that are not as parallel as they can be. Sometimes, the best idea is to rewrite the sentence as two sentences.

- Here's a sentence:

  They have a vacation home, two cars and are planning a trip to Africa.

- The last part is not parallel. It's possible to rewrite that sentence so it has parallel parts:

  They have a vacation home, two cars and a plan for going to Africa.

- The last part is parallel.

- Another way to fix up the sentence is to write it as two sentences. You can use this way if you can't think of wording that makes the parts parallel.

- Here's the sentence rewritten as two sentences:

  They have a vacation home and two cars. They are planning a trip to Africa.

- The second sentence doesn't have to be parallel to the first.

Part C | Rewrite each sentence as two sentences.

1. The students could read music, sing well and had good rhythm.

2. Mary constructs porches, bathrooms and is a good carpenter.

3. Their house has two bathrooms, a large recreation room and is located near a good school.

4. Robert has five sisters, two dogs and likes to fish.

5. That dog barks at night, digs holes in the yard and chewed up all the furniture last year.

Part D | Follow the outline diagram and tell how the two things named in the equal boxes are the same.

Outline diagram

[taking a trip] **=** [reading a good book]

Part E | These sentences are passive. Rewrite them so they are active.

1. The committee was formed by Ms. Anderson.
2. That article was written by a professor of mathematics.
3. A warning was given by the leader of the group.
4. The passage was rewritten by her.
5. The report was criticized by one of the students.

Part F Follow the outline diagram to write about the problem with each argument.

Argument 1: The sign in front of Fireside Restaurant is very unattractive. The food served in that restaurant must be unattractive and tasteless.

Argument 2: Fran must spend days completing one of her paintings. I watched her paint a small detail, and it took her more than 10 minutes.

Argument 3: I visited two doctors who have offices in the Ferris Building. They were excellent. Therefore, all the other doctors in that building must be excellent.

Outline diagram

Argument ___ uses evidence about _____ to draw a conclusion about _____.

However, evidence about _____ does not lead to a proper conclusion about _____.

Part G Write each sentence with the correct last word. Indicate the part of the speech of the last word.

1. Rodney reminded his brother to drive _____.

   | safe | | safely |

2. Those birds sounded _____.

   | loud | | loudly |

3. Her jacket felt _____.

   | smooth | | smoothly |

4. The engine ran _____.

   | smooth | | smoothly |

5. The air in the garden was _____.

   | fragrant | | fragrantly |

Lesson  64

- Some sentences are sort of parallel. You could interpret these sentences as if they give parallel meanings. Or you could argue that they do not give parallel meanings. In some situations, these sentences are unclear.

- Here's an example:

  They collected old coins and jewels.

- That sentence could mean that the coins are old and the jewels are old. Or that sentence could mean that the coins are old but the jewels are not necessarily old.

- If both the coins and jewels are old, you could rewrite the sentence this way:

  They collected old coins and old jewels.

- If only the coins are old, you could rewrite the sentence this way:

  They collected jewels and old coins.

- The sentence is clear because **old coins** is last.

Rewrite each sentence two ways—one way for each picture.

Item 1:   The chair had a torn seat and arms.

 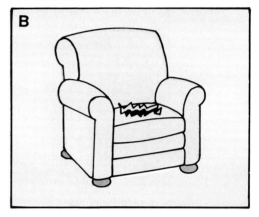

Item 2:   The dog had large ears and spots.

 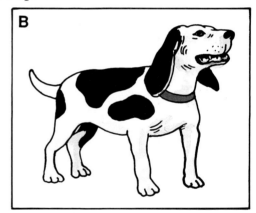

Item 3:   We observed angry chipmunks and robins.

Part C

- Here are some sentences that are not clear when they stand by themselves:

  That was tiring.

  This doesn't make any sense.

- For the first sentence, we could ask: **What was tiring?**

- For the second sentence, we could ask: **What doesn't make any sense?**

- As a rule, the **name** should follow the words **this** or **that.**

- Here are the sentences fixed up:

  That <u>trip</u> was tiring.

  This <u>argument</u> doesn't make any sense.

- Remember, **this** and **that** need a noun after them.

Part D

Sample Item

Tracy's suggestion was to call the garage. <u>The problem with this was that the garage was closed.</u>

The second sentence should say:

The problem with this **suggestion** was that the garage was closed.

For each item, rewrite the second sentence so it is perfectly clear.

1. They decided to complain about the noise. <u>They wanted this to cause some action.</u>

2. They finally decided to buy the mountain bike. <u>It took them two weeks to arrive at this.</u>

3. Tom recommended that we should bring along work clothes. <u>Randy did not agree with this.</u>

Rewrite each sentence that is passive so that it is active.

Passage

¹ The Dunn Company decided to purchase a new copy machine. ² The decision was made by a committee. ³ The committee recommended the Stinmore copy machine. ⁴ This recommendation was rejected by Miss Thompson. ⁵ The Reemto copier was preferred by Miss Thompson. ⁶ The committee recommended firing Miss Thompson. ⁷ Miss Thompson recommended firing the committee. ⁸ A meeting was ordered by the president of the Dunn Company. ⁹ The president ordered the committee to work with Miss Thompson. ¹⁰ The president told everybody to agree on one copy machine. ¹¹ The committee met with Miss Thompson five times. ¹² The name of the chosen machine was announced by the committee. ¹³ The Dunn Company purchased a Bleepo copier.

Part F Follow the outline diagram to explain the problem with the argument.

Argument:

A recent study showed that children who perform better in school come from families that have two or more telephones. Dr. Reemore conducted this study and pointed out that "the very best students not only had three phones in the house, but also had car phones." The study clearly documents that students who come from homes that have no phones do not do well in school. As Dr. Reemore observed, "We studied some homeless families with no phones. Students from these families did not do well in school."

Outline diagram

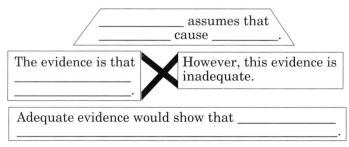

Part G | Follow the outline diagram to write about the problem with each argument.

Argument 1: We saw the part of the iceburg that was above the water. It was about 50 feet high. So, the part that was under the water must have been about the same depth, 50 feet.

Argument 2: I know that Mr. Jenson is a very nervous person with nervous behaviors. I saw him give a speech, and he was nervous.

Argument 3: I know that Wednesday was a beautiful day in Casper, Wyoming. I was there in the morning, and let me tell you—it was beautiful.

Outline diagram

Argument __ uses evidence about _____ to draw a conclusion about _____.

However, evidence about _____ does not lead to a proper conclusion about _____.

Follow the outline diagram to write about the problem with these directions.

Directions: Make a shape that is one inch high.
Write a letter above that shape.

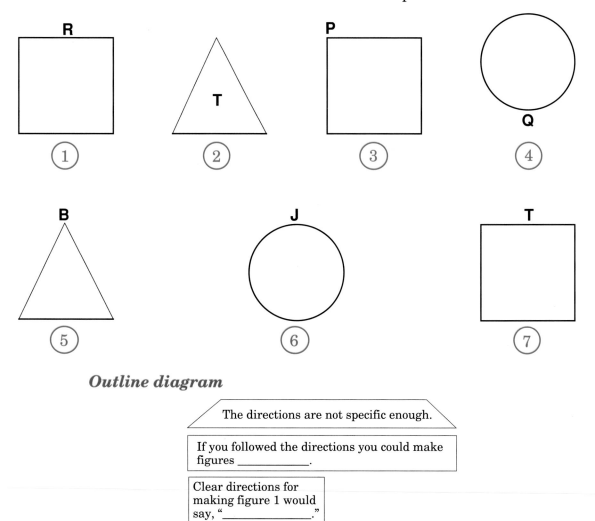

Outline diagram

The directions are not specific enough.

If you followed the directions you could make figures _____.

Clear directions for making figure 1 would say, "_____."

Clear directions for making figure 3 would say, "_____."

Part A | Rewrite each sentence two ways—one way for each picture.

Item 1: The room had new rugs and skylights.

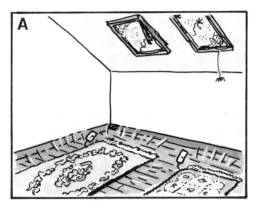 

Item 2: We visited a neighborhood with tall buildings and trees.

Item 3: That store sells used furniture and carpeting.

For each item, rewrite the second sentence so it is perfectly clear.

1. Luisa proposed that we would study together. <u>I didn't find this acceptable.</u>

2. Tanika suggested that we should save 200 dollars. <u>Nobody agreed with this.</u>

3. Larry argued that we should take the bus to the park. <u>Carlos agreed that this made a lot of sense.</u>

Rewrite each passive sentence so that it is active.

Passage

¹ Mrs. Lee told her students to decide on a class project. ² Seven projects were considered by the class. ³ The class voted on those projects three times. ⁴ Two projects were ruled out by the first vote. ⁵ The second vote ruled out one more project. ⁶ The class announced its choice by making a sign. ⁷ The sign said, "Keep our rivers clean." ⁸ The class was going to clean up a section of the Muddy River. ⁹ Bags and tools were donated by parents. ¹⁰ The students were transported to the river by three trucks. ¹¹ The students spent all day Saturday and Sunday picking up garbage. ¹² They were photographed by a reporter. ¹³ An article about the clean-up appeared in the Wednesday newspaper. ¹⁴ The class was pleased by that article.

Follow the outline diagram to explain the problem with the argument.

Dianne Olson's argument

My neighbor, Bill Anderson, has a simple way of avoiding car problems. Every day, before he gets into his car, he pats it three times on the roof. Bill's car hasn't had a problem in over 120,000 miles. I've had lots of car problems in the last year, but I'm going to start patting my car.

Outline diagram

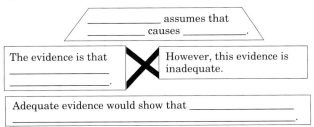

Independent Work

Part E | Write about the problem with each of these arguments.

Argument 1: Fran must be very nervous when she speaks in front of a group. I saw her just before she was going to the dentist's office, and she was extremely nervous.

Argument 2: I know that Dennis must be very good at everything that involves using his hands. I saw him take an engine apart, and he was awesome. His hands moved like streaks of lightning.

Outline diagram

| Argument ___ uses evidence about _____'s behavior while _____ to draw a conclusion about _____. | | However, evidence about _____ does not lead to a proper conclusion about _____. |

Rewrite each sentence that has a silly meaning.

1. Our dog can eat more than our three cats.
2. Our dog eats more than two cans of dog food each day.
3. The vacuum cleaner picked up more than the fleas.
4. Our house contains a lot more junk than Andy's house.
5. The cook prepared more than the waiter.
6. Our class observed more than the students in Ms. Anderson's class.
7. Last year's vacation was longer than this year's vacation.
8. My brother washed more than the car.

Lesson 66

- Sometimes we write sentences that tell what people think, prefer or feel. Some of the sentences we write may have a silly meaning.

- Here's a sentence:

  Milton's thought was making a new fence.

- Here's a picture of the silly meaning:

- There are three ways to fix up this sentence.

- One way is to use the word **that.**

- Here's the sentence about Milton's thought:

  Milton's thought was that we should make a fence.

- A second way is to get rid of the verb with **I–N–G** and replace it with a verb that tells what **to do:**

  Milton's thought was to make a new fence.

- The third way is to exchange the noun **thought** for a related verb:

  Milton thought that we should build a new fence.

Rewrite the second sentence in each item two ways: 1) replace the verb that ends with **I-N-G** with a verb that tells what **to do;** 2) exchange the noun in the subject for a verb.

1. Somebody asked where we preferred to eat dinner. Brenda's preference was sitting on the patio.

2. Somebody asked how we would pay for the repairs. Ms. Wilson's feeling was borrowing money.

| For each item, rewrite the second sentence so it is perfectly clear.

1. Dianne asked the senator how he planned to reduce crime.
   <u>I felt that this got right to the point.</u>

2. Rose figured out a way to make cups without handles. <u>I used
   that to make three cups.</u>

3. The ad indicated that Bumpos are the best cars on the road.
   <u>Dr. Nelson didn't agree with this.</u>

| For each item, write a combined sentence that uses **who, which** or **that.** Label the part of speech for each word.

1. *This part is essential:*
   I bought a new bike.
   This part is essential:
   It has mud tires.

2. *This part is essential:*
   She painted a beautiful picture.
   This part is not essential:
   It showed a blue lake.

3. *This part is essential:*
   We watched a hydrofoil.
   This part is not essential:
   It is a fast boat.

4. *This part is essential:*
   Our neighbor is a paleontologist.
   This part is essential:
   She studies dinosaur remains.

Part E

- Here's a slogan that is often true:

  You can make numbers lie.

- Here's a case where the numbers lie:

  In April, the Bumpo Automobile Company sold 12 cars throughout the world. During May, the company sold 30 cars.

- Here is how the president of Bumpo explained the company's success:

  "During May, we more than doubled our sales, compared to the month before."

- The statement is true, but doubling 12 is not very impressive. Doubling something like 5,000 would be impressive.

Part F | Follow the outline diagram to write about the problem with the claim.

Here are the facts:

The Edison 5th graders were compared with the Morrison 5th graders in math. Here is a list of the top eight students:

Billy J.	Edison
Keisha F.	Morrison
Jean K.	Morrison
Allen P.	Morrison
Clinton G.	Morrison
Rosa T.	Morrison
Frank M.	Morrison
Soon-Yee L.	Morrison

Here's what the math teacher from Edison wrote:

When our students were compared with the students at Morrison, the very highest score was held by a student from Edison. Edison, therefore, has a superior math program.

Outline diagram

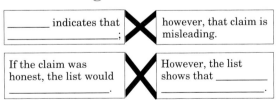

Part G Follow the appropriate outline diagram to write about the problem with each argument.

> **Argument 1:** Aunt Henna has a wonderful cure for colds. She fixes her herb soup and has you drink a small bowl of it two times a day for five or six days. The cold almost always goes away by the end of the sixth day.

> **Argument 2:** Donna must be a very fast reader. I noticed that she talks and runs fast. She is just one of those persons with fast behavior.

Outline diagrams

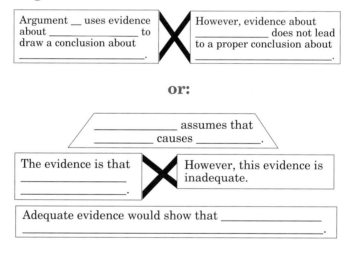

or:

Part H All the sentences below are passive. Rewrite each sentence so it is active.

1. The book was returned by Mark and his sister.

2. The decision was made by the committee to widen Main Street.

3. That car is driven by our neighbor, Bob Dixon.

4. Twelve fish were eaten by the seals.

Follow the outline diagram and tell how the two things named in the equal boxes are the same.

Outline diagram

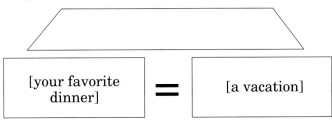

| [your favorite dinner] | **=** | [a vacation] |

Lesson 67

Rewrite the second sentence in each item two ways: 1) replace the verb that ends with **I-N-G** with a verb that tells what **to do;** 2) exchange the noun in the subject for a verb.

1. Somebody asked what we should do after the game. <u>Yolanda's suggestion was eating pizza.</u>

2. Somebody asked how we could get across the river. <u>Ron's plan was taking a rubber raft with us.</u>

3. Somebody asked how far we could get on the first day of our vacation. <u>Laura's hope was getting all the way to Idaho.</u>

Part B

Rewrite the entire passage so it is clear. Every sentence has at least one problem.

It was decided by the school council to clean up another part of the Muddy River. Mr. Parson's idea was taking rafts down the river. Another idea was to wade in the river, drag chains, and the chains would collect junk. This was not accepted by the council. Some objections of the council was strong. Heidi's idea was wearing bright colors and life jackets, but we did not have enough life jackets. James thought that everybody should wear heavy gloves and hats.

- Some sentences use the word **they** in a way that is not clear.
- Here's a sentence:
    They opened a new store on the corner.
- The word **they** doesn't really refer to anybody. So we rewrite the sentence so it does not use the word **they:**
    A new store opened on the corner.
- Sometimes we have more information for rewriting the sentence.
- Here are two sentences:
    The City Council meets today.
    They won't make any decisions.
- The council isn't a **they,** but an **it.**
- Here's the correct sentence:
    It won't make any decisions.

Rewrite the second sentence in each item so it is clear.

1. The bank opened its new parking lot. <u>They also gave away balloons.</u>

2. The company purchased new trucks. <u>They painted them red.</u>

Part E | Follow the outline diagram to write about the problem with the ad.

Eatmore ad

Hey gang,

Isn't it time for you to switch to **Eatmore** and start getting more for your money? That's right, for the same price you'd pay for 25 pieces of Yum-Yum, you can enjoy 35 pieces of delicious **Eatmore**. That's what I call yum yum.

Table F16

	Number of pieces per bag	Size of pieces	Weight	Cost
Eatmore	35	$\frac{1}{4}$ inch dots	1 pound	$2.89
Yum-Yum	25	1 inch squares	1 pound, 3 ounces	$2.89

Outline diagram

_____ indicates that _____;	however, that claim is misleading.

If the claim was honest, Table __ would indicate _____ _____.	However, the table indicates that _____ _____ _____.

Part F | Rewrite each sentence two ways—one way for each picture.

Item 1:   The cats had brown eyes and collars.

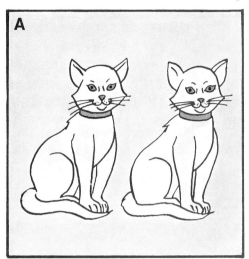
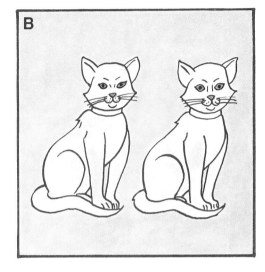

Item 2:   We saw tall women and men at the party.

Follow the appropriate outline diagram to write about each argument.

Argument 1: The new auditorium cost much more than the city thought it would cost. The seats inside the auditorium must be far more expensive than they should be.

Argument 2: Andy is afraid of getting bitten by rattlesnakes. He figured out a way to keep them away. He laid a rope all the way around his yard. It's been 15 years and no rattlesnakes have been seen in his yard—or in the rest of the city, for that matter. The rope trick is very effective.

Outline diagrams

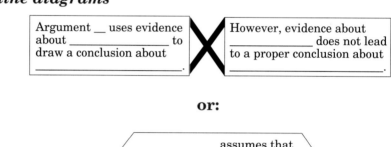

Argument ___ uses evidence about _____ to draw a conclusion about _____.

However, evidence about _____ does not lead to a proper conclusion about _____.

or:

_____ assumes that _____ causes _____.

The evidence is that _____ _____.

However, this evidence is inadequate.

Adequate evidence would show that _____ _____.

Part A | For each item, rewrite the second sentence so it is clear.

1. Somebody asked how we could get that piano up the front stairs. <u>Jane's idea was building a ramp.</u>

2. Somebody asked what we should do at our next meeting. <u>Keith's choice was planning the Christmas party.</u>

Part B   **Bumpo Ad**

Summary Table
Miles Per Tank of Gas

	City	Flat country	Mountains
Dennis 350	280 miles	588 miles	406 miles
Bumpo Free Spirit	289 miles	595 miles	408 miles

Use the information in the specifications and follow the outline diagram to write about the problem with the claim.

Specifications

	Weight	Horsepower	Fuel tank	Price
Dennis 350	3,205 pounds	165	14 gallons	$37,500
Bumpo Free Spirit	2,988 pounds	165	17 gallons	$36,088

Outline diagram

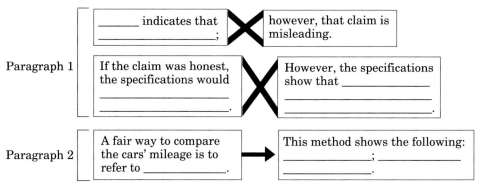

Paragraph 1

_____ indicates that _____ ;

however, that claim is misleading.

If the claim was honest, the specifications would _____ _____ .

However, the specifications show that _____ _____ .

Paragraph 2

A fair way to compare the cars' mileage is to refer to _____ .

This method shows the following: _____ ; _____ _____ .

Part D Rewrite the entire passage so it is clear.

Heavy black work gloves were donated by Feebo Hardware Store. They also loaned the school three heavy chains. Mr. Ferguson gave a talk on how to wade safely in the Muddy. Dr. Smith warned us about walking on broken bottles and rocks. On Friday, we received the news that parts of the Muddy River was flooding. The project was cancelled by the school council.

Part E | Rewrite each sentence so it is active.

1. Mr. Jenkins was congratulated by the president for doing a good job.

2. Our house will be painted by the Redmore Construction Company.

3. Our dog was attacked by Emory, the neighbor's police dog.

4. The best paper was written by Agnes.

Part F | Follow the appropriate outline diagram to write about the argument.

Argument: I watched the first part of the nature program on channel 12. It was so boring that I knew the whole thing would be boring. So I turned it off and watched something else.

Outline diagrams

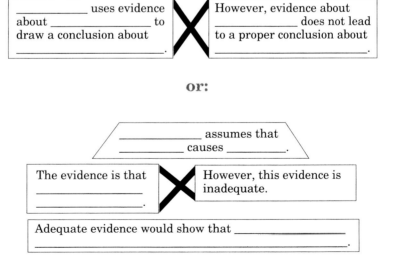

Follow the outline diagram to write about the problem with these directions. Write specific directions for making figures A and D.

Directions: Make a rectangle that is 1 inch wide.
Write the letter R inside the rectangle.

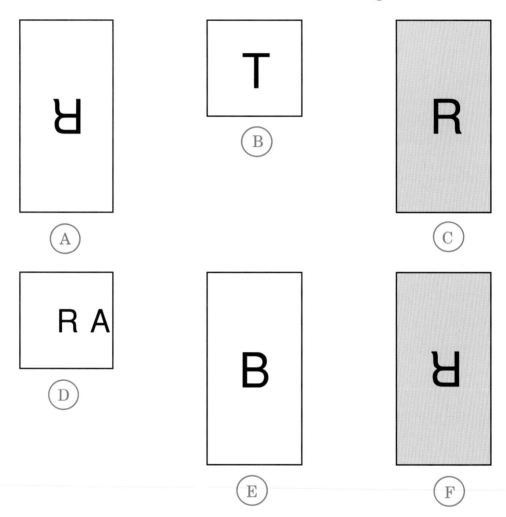

Outline diagram

The directions are not specific enough.

If you followed the directions, you could make figures _____ .

Clear directions for making figure ___ would say, "_____."

Clear directions for making figure ___ would say, "_____."

Part A

- You're going to do some projects that involve parts of speech. You've seen that words have different parts of speech in different sentences. You figure out the part of speech by seeing where the word is and what the word does.

- Sometimes the word **remaining** is a verb:

    The girls were remaining in the office.

- It's a verb because it tells what the girls were doing.

- Sometimes the same word is an adjective:

    We didn't eat the remaining fish.

- **Remaining** is an adjective because it comes before **fish** and tells what kind of fish.

- You've learned about joining words: **and, or** and **but.** These words are **conjunctions.**

- Other words can be conjunctions in some sentences.

- Here's how you test to see if a word is a conjunction:
    - ✔ If the words that follow it make a complete sentence, the word is a conjunction.

- The word **that** is a conjunction in some sentences.

- Here is one of those sentences:

    She argued that <u>her brother should help her clean the garage.</u>

- The words after the word **that** are underlined. They make up a complete sentence:

    Her brother should help her clean the garage.

- The word **that** is a conjunction in that sentence.

- The word **that** is not a conjunction in this sentence:

    He bought a car that <u>was red.</u>

- The words after **that** do not make up a complete sentence. So **that** is not a conjunction.

For each item, indicate whether the word **that** is a conjunction or a pronoun.

1. He believed that <u>we would win the game.</u>

2. He bought a house that <u>had a large basement.</u>

3. Brown Company is the one that <u>gives the best service.</u>

4. I wish that <u>she had invited me.</u>

Use the information in the table and follow the outline diagram to write about the problem with the claim.

Press release from the Stinger Sewing Machine Company:

Recently, our latest Stinger, the Busy Bee 2000, was compared with the best-selling machine, the Hummer 1000. The Stinger soundly outperformed the Hummer. After 16,000 hours of continuous running, the Stinger machine required only five repairs. During the same number of hours, the Hummer required eight repairs. Clearly, the Stinger is a more reliable machine than the Hummer.

Table F17

Sewing Machine	Hours of Use	Number of Repairs
Stinger Busy Bee 2000	16,000	5
Hummer 1000	16,000	8

Table F18
Actual Data: Number of Hours, Number of Repairs and Type of Fabric

Sewing Machine	On Thin Fabric		On Thick Fabric	
	Hours of Use	Number of Repairs	Hours of Use	Number of Repairs
Stinger Busy Bee 2000	16,000	5	11,700	6
Hummer 1000	12,000	3	16,000	8

Outline diagram

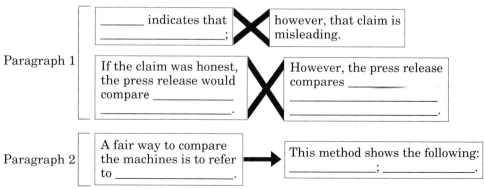

Paragraph 1

_____ indicates that _____;

however, that claim is misleading.

If the claim was honest, the press release would compare _____ _____.

However, the press release compares _____ _____ _____.

Paragraph 2

A fair way to compare the machines is to refer to _____.

This method shows the following: _____; _____.

Part D | For each item, write a combined sentence that uses **who, which** or **that.** Then label the part of speech for each word.

1. *This part is essential:*
   I followed the path.
   This part is not essential:
   It was steep.

2. *This part is essential:*
   We heard three speeches.
   This part is essential:
   They were short, but interesting.

3. *This part is essential:*
   I visited my cousin.
   This part is essential:
   She has five dogs.

Part E | Rewrite the second sentence in each item so the meaning is clear.

1. Mary didn't want to drive to the park. Her suggestion was riding the bus.

2. Dan didn't accept the teacher's explanation. His strategy was arguing for more evidence.

3. The students were deciding what to do. Fran's choice was playing soccer instead of swimming.

Follow the appropriate outline diagram to write about the problem with each argument.

Argument 1: Mr. Ferguson's argument began with a very complicated explanation. I stopped listening, but I know that his conclusion must have been so complicated that nobody could understand it.

Argument 2: Ms. Taylor has a wonderful method of making little purple flowers appear every spring. She waits until the end of March. Then she sprinkles the ashes of burnt wood all around her flower bed. Within a week or two, hundreds of beautiful purple flowers appear.

Outline diagrams

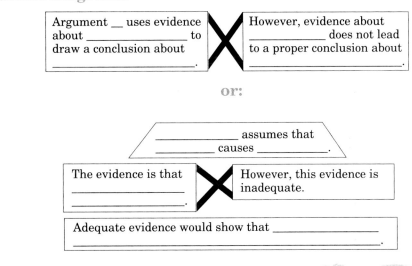

Argument __ uses evidence about _____ to draw a conclusion about _____.

However, evidence about _____ does not lead to a proper conclusion about _____.

or:

_____ assumes that _____ causes _____.

The evidence is that _____ _____.

However, this evidence is inadequate.

Adequate evidence would show that _____ _____.

Lesson 70 – Test 7

Part A | These sentences are passive. Rewrite them so they are active.

1. Mr. Erving was injured by a falling branch.

2. My doctor was called at least three times last week by Mrs. Franklin.

3. Dennis was defeated by Vern, who is the new champion.

Part B | Rewrite each sentence so all the parts are parallel or make the sentence into two sentences.

1. Our house is spacious, warm and has three skylights.

2. Her behavior was playful, humorous and had a lot of energy.

Follow the appropriate outline diagram to write about the problem with each argument.

Argument 1: We noticed that students who wear red do better on tests than students who do not wear red. We are telling all our students to wear red next week when they have their reading tests. I'm sure they will do much better than they ever have done before.

Argument 2: The steering wheel in the Bumpo 6000 is made of a very expensive material. I know that the wheels on the Bumpo must also be made of expensive material.

Argument 3: Martha's cousin Darby must be a very slow person. He drove us to the airport, and he drove so slowly that we almost missed our plane. He must be terrible at anything that requires fast actions.

Argument 4: Mr. Jenkins has three roosters that have a remarkable power. They actually make the sun come up in the morning. They start crowing when it is still dark, and the first thing you know, the sun comes up. I just hope that he keeps those roosters. Imagine how dark it would be all the time if they didn't bring the sun up by crowing.

Outline diagrams

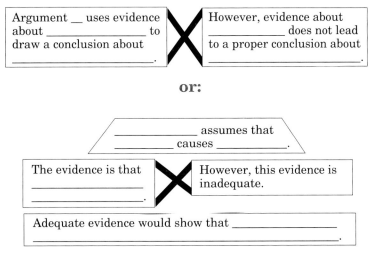

For each item, rewrite the second sentence so it is clear.

1. The garage was a complete mess. My recommendation was having a garage sale.

2. Our dog barks at night, and she is creating some serious problems. My idea is letting her sleep with me.

Team
Activities

Lesson 71 – Team Activity

Part A

- You've worked with the word **that.**

- The word **that** can be an adjective if it tells what kind or how many:

    That boy is busy.

- The word **that** can be a pronoun if it replaces another pronoun:

    I bought a bike that **had mud tires.**

- The word **that** replaces **it:**

    It had mud tires.

- The word **that** can also be a conjunction. If the words following **that** make up a complete sentence, the word **that** is a conjunction.

- There are other words that work the same way. You're going to show that other words are conjunctions in some sentences.

- Here are two words that can be conjunctions:

    before   because

Part B   Write two complete sentences that show that **before** and **because** are conjunctions.

Part C   *Team Activity*

- Identify as many different conjunctions as you can. Illustrate that the words you identified are conjunctions by showing them in sentences.

- These are words you can't use:

    and   but   or   therefore   however   nevertheless

- Write an argument that starts with the rule for conjunctions and then lists the words you think are conjunctions. For each word, present a sentence as evidence. Explain why the word is a conjunction in your sentence.

Lesson 72 – Team Activity

TV Should Be Banned for Young People
by
Dr. H.S. Geiger

Young people under 18 years old should never watch TV. There are three reasons for banning TV.

First of all, watching TV will cause poor health. Here is why: People who are in poor health watch TV more than people who are in good health. Therefore, watching TV a lot must cause poor health.

Second, watching TV programs causes young people to become violent. Many TV programs are full of violence. Young people who are violent watch violent TV programs. Therefore, any young person will learn to become violent by watching TV.

Finally, if parents prohibited youngsters from watching TV, our community would be a much better place. Here's why: Youngsters would have more free time. They would have to do something with this free time. Therefore, they would decide to do useful things. So they would spend time helping the homeless, doing extra things around school and participating in community activities.

For all these reasons, kids under 18 should never be allowed to watch TV.

Part B | Make an outline diagram and write a report that explains the problems with Dr. Geiger's evidence.

- Dr. Geiger gives three reasons for his conclusion. You might repeat part of the diagram for each reason.

- You'll need a summary statement at the beginning.

- You could express your opinion at the end. Tell how you feel about the sensible use of TV.

- The whole passage should be at least five paragraphs long.

- Your team could assign different parts of the passage to different students.

Lesson 73 – Team Activity

Outline diagram

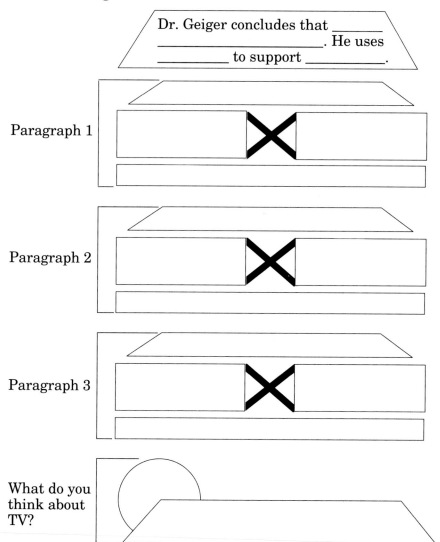

Dr. Geiger concludes that _____ _____. He uses _____ to support _____.

Paragraph 1

Paragraph 2

Paragraph 3

What do you think about TV?

Lessons 74 and 75 – Team Activity

- You're going to prove that some arguments are misleading. You'll do that by making up an actual example that uses more-complete evidence than the argument does but that contradicts the conclusion.

- If you show that the more-complete evidence leads to the opposite conclusion, you show that the argument is unsound or misleading.

Here's a conclusion that Dave drew:

10-year-old boys are taller than 10-year-old girls.

Here's Dave's evidence for this conclusion:

I recorded the height of the four tallest 10-year-olds in a classroom. Three of those students were boys. Therefore, 10-years-old boys are taller than 10-year-old girls.

Phase 1: Class list

Make up heights for all the students in a classroom of 26 students. Show the evidence so it shows Dave's evidence, but show the evidence so it does not support Dave's conclusion.

Show

- Three of the four tallest children are boys.
- The girls are taller than the boys.

Phase 2: Outline diagram

Make up an outline diagram for writing about the problem with Dave's argument.

Phase 3: Passages

Follow your outline diagram to write a clear report. Use your evidence on the class you made up to show that Dave's evidence is very misleading.

Student	Height	Sex
A		
B		
C		
D		
E		
F		
G		
H		
I		
J		
K		
L		
M		
N		
O		
P		
Q		
R		
S		
T		
U		
V		
W		
X		
Y		
Z		

Lesson 76 – Team Activity

Part A

- You've worked with essential parts and nonessential parts of sentences. A part that is not essential is set off with commas.

- There are a few **conjunctions** that **always introduce nonessential parts.**

- One of those conjunctions is **although.** No matter where you place the part that begins with **although,** you must set off that part with a comma:

  <u>Although</u> he was tired, he kept on working.

  He kept on working, <u>although</u> he was tired.

Part B

- At least one other conjunction works like **although.** That word is never used with an essential part.

- You'll figure out which word that might be.

- You'll write an argument that uses evidence to support your choice.

Lessons 77 and 78 – Team Activity

Mr. Taylor's argument:

I told some children facts about the continents. They didn't remember the facts that I told them.

I told some other children how to work long-division problems. They didn't learn long division.

I told some other children how to repair a washing machine. They didn't learn from what I told them.

Therefore, I have come to the conclusion that children do not learn anything that people tell them. They must learn in some other mysterious ways.

Phase 1: **List other possibilities**

1. Children can't learn from anything people tell them.

2.

3.

4.

Phase 2: **Design a test**

Decide what kind of explainers, topics and children you would need in a test to rule out other possible explanations.

- Decide what kind of children.
- Decide what kind of explainers.
- Decide three more things to teach.

Table F19

Explainers	Topics	200 children
Mr. Taylor	a. Facts about continents	
	b. Long division	? High
___?___	c. Repairing a washing machine	
	d. _____?	? Average
___?___	e. _____?	
	f. _____?	? Low

Phase 3:   **Possible outcomes**

Make up a table that shows possible outcomes.

- Which children succeed?
- Which explainers succeed?
- Which topics succeed?

Conclusion: **Outcomes that support:**

1. Children can't learn from explanations.

2. The material Mr. Taylor presented was too difficult.

3. The children Mr. Taylor worked with were not typical.

4. Mr. Taylor is a bad explainer.

Phase 4:   **Write**

Follow the outline diagram to write about the problems with Mr. Taylor's argument.

Outline diagram

_____ concludes _____
_____.

The evidence for his conclusion _____
_____.

However, this evidence supports three other possible conclusions:
_____; _____; _____.

[Describe each test. Which teachers? Which topics? Which student?]

If _____
the outcome would support
_____.

If _____
the outcome would discredit
_____.

We believe _____
_____.

Lessons 79 and 80 – Team Activity

> **Mr. Grover wrote this:**
>
> We are very distressed about the increasing rate of traffic accidents in our town. At the end of 1990, the town passed regulations that were supposed to increase safety on the streets. The cost of enforcing these regulations is over $100,000 a year.
>
> Have the regulations done any good? No. A recent report by the state shows that the number of accidents in Tintown has increased a lot. In 1990, we had only 5 accidents in the town. The number of accidents has gone up every year since then. In 1994, there were 13 accidents. That's more than 2 times the number of accidents that occurred in 1990.
>
> So here's the bottom line: We are paying big bucks for regulations that are supposed to reduce traffic accidents; however, it is very clear that those regulations **cause more accidents to occur.** I say that we should get rid of the regulations and stop kidding ourselves into thinking they work.

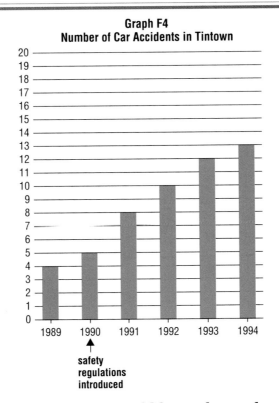

Graph F4
Number of Car Accidents in Tintown

Phase 1: List the ways Tintown could have changed so you would expect more accidents even if the regulations were very effective.

Phase 2: Graph F5 shows more evidence. Use the form shown in graph F6 to graph the number of miles per accident in Tintown.

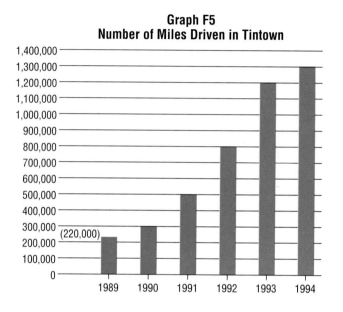

Graph F5
Number of Miles Driven in Tintown

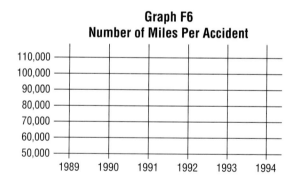

Graph F6
Number of Miles Per Accident

Phase 3: Write a thoughtful response to Mr. Grover's argument.

- First summarize Mr. Grover's argument by telling his conclusion.

- Then tell the problems with his argument. Present your graph and explain it.

- Draw your own conclusion about whether or not the safety regulations are effective.

Student
Answer Key

Answer Key

Lesson 1

Part B

3. one argument
4. some water
5. some seeds
8. some events
9. some noise
12. one sister

Part G

Sample: A sora is a small, short-billed rail of North America.

1. A manifold is a chamber that has several outlets through which a liquid or gas is distributed or gathered.
2. An insidious person or thing looks harmless but actually causes harm.
3. Something terse is straight to the point without apology.

Lesson 2

Part D

1. A person who is demure is shy and modest.
2. A calumnious person is sly and full of tricks.
3. A hexagon is a figure with six sides and six angles.

Lesson 7

Part E

1. The dogs ran faster than the children ran.
2. Wayne suffered more from the cold than from the wind.
3. They put more gas in the tractor than in the truck.
4. The horse weighed more than the cow weighed.
5. Diane crawls faster than Frances crawls.
6. The wind blew faster from the west than from the north.

Lesson 8

Part A

1. The heater made more noise than the radio made.
2. The watch kept better time than the clock kept.
3. The temperature was higher in the morning than in the afternoon.
4. They would rather go with Ted than with Margaret.
5. My uncle drives faster than my mother drives.
6. The wallpaper looks prettier in yellow than in orange.

Lesson 9

Part C

1. Tina painted faster than her father painted.
2. Freddie ate less than the rest of the students ate.
5. She walked faster to the store than to the school.
7. More rain fell in the morning than in the evening.
8. The lily smelled better than the rose smelled.

Lesson 12

Part D

1. She painted more than the floor painted. **silly**

2. She threw more than a dozen stones threw. **silly**

3. Tom read more books than his sister read.

4. Rosa read more than the magazines read. **silly**

5. She collected less than her sisters collected.

6. Tigers sleep longer than dogs sleep.

Lesson 16

Part A

1. Y; present
2. X; present
3. X; present
4. Z; past
5. Z; future
6. X; present

Lesson 17

Part C

These sentences are not very good:

Pets A, C, H, I and J discredit rule 1 because **they have pointed heads.**

Pets A, C, H, I and J discredit rule 1 because they are bald but are different from what rule 1 says.

Lesson 18

Part B

1. X; past
2. X; present
3. Z; past
4. Z; future
5. Z; past
6. X; past

Lesson 19

Part D

Here are sentences that are not too good:

1. However, if Mrs. Johnson examined a larger sample of pets, she might find a pet with a pointed head.

2. However, if Mrs. Johnson examined a larger sample of pets, she might find a pet that doesn't have a tail with a pointed head.

Lesson 22

Part C

1. Does the paper have small spaces between the lines?

2. Does the paper have more than one margin?

3. Does the paper have a margin on the right side?

Lesson 28

Part C

1. was—past
2. are—present
3. will help—future
4. makes—present
5. is—present
6. are—present
7. can help—present

Lesson 26

Part B

*Suddenly, the bridge **tilts** to one side.*
Suddenly, the bridge **tilted** to one side.

*Andrew almost **falls** off.*
Andrew almost **fell** off.

*He **grabs** Linda.*
He **grabbed** Linda.

*In the meantime, Andrew **is losing** his grip on the rail.*
In the meantime, Andrew **was losing** his grip on the rail.

Lesson 28

Part D

Doctor	Annual earnings	Type of house	Vehicles that doctor owns	Type of neighborhood
Dr. Marks	$125,000	large, expensive	2 cars, a boat	very nice
Dr. Ukimo	$35,000	small hut	bicycle	poor
Dr. Jones	$200,000	very large, very expensive	3 cars, a yacht	ritzy
Dr. Johnson	$80,000	average	1 car	nice

Doctor	Annual earnings	Type of house	Vehicles that doctor owns	Type of neighborhood
Dr. Marks	$125,000	large, expensive	2 cars, a boat	very nice
Dr. Ukimo	$35,000	small hut	an old car	simple
Dr. Jones	$150,000	very large, very expensive	2 cars, a boat 3 motorcycles	fancy
Dr. Johnson	$100,000	average	2 cars	nice

Lesson 29

Part D

Location	Distance	Airfare	Rooms	Hotel grounds and view	Total cost for 4 people, 3 days (including airfare)
Point Vista	450 miles	$450	very large	excellent	$1000
Point Terra	900 miles	$900	very large	excellent	$1500
Point Hope	200 miles	$200	tiny	okay	$500
Point Away	800 miles	$800	luxurious	elegant	$3000

Location	Distance	Airfare	Rooms	Hotel grounds and view	Total cost for 4 people, 3 days (including airfare)
Point Vista	450 miles	$450	very large	excellent	$1000
Point Terra	900 miles	$900	quite large	very nice	$1500
Point Hope	200 miles	$200	tiny	okay	$450
Point Away	800 miles	$800	huge	the finest	$3000

Lesson 31

Part D

```
         V       AV
1.  barked yesterday

         V    AV
2.  looked east

          V      N
3.  watched animals      them

        V      AV
4.  went home
```

```
          V       N
5.  bought milk        it

          V      N
6.  watched birds      them

        V    AV
7.  looked up

         V    AV
8.  traveled alone
```

Lesson 32

Part A

1. <u>had</u> (V) <u>adventures</u> (N)   them
2. <u>splashed</u> (V) <u>water</u> (N)   it
3. <u>played</u> (V) <u>vigorously</u> (AV)
4. <u>sang</u> (V) <u>songs</u> (N)   them
5. <u>sang</u> (V) <u>loudly</u> (AV)
6. <u>came</u> (V) <u>later</u> (AV)
7. <u>loves</u> (V) <u>watermelons</u> (N)   them
8. <u>develop</u> (V) <u>strength</u> (N)   it

Lesson 33

Part F

1. <u>interesting</u> (A) <u>picture</u> (N)
2. <u>around</u> (AV) <u>birds</u> (N)
3. <u>beautiful</u> (A) <u>birds</u> (N)
4. <u>difficult</u> (A) <u>work</u> (N)
5. <u>longer</u> (A) <u>shadows</u> (N)
6. <u>down</u> (AV) <u>sun</u> (N)
7. <u>here</u> (AV) <u>children</u> (N)
8. <u>complicated</u> (A) <u>sentences</u> (N)
9. <u>together</u> (AV) <u>birds</u> (N)
10. <u>tired</u> (A) <u>workers</u> (N)

Lesson 34

Part C

1. <u>unfriendly</u> (A) <u>dog</u> (N)
2. <u>fiercely</u> (AV) <u>dog</u> (N)
3. <u>outside</u> (AV) <u>girls</u> (N)
4. <u>enormous</u> (A) <u>buildings</u> (N)
5. <u>softly</u> (AV) <u>snow</u> (N)
6. <u>good</u> (A) <u>argument</u> (N)
7. <u>together</u> (AV) <u>groups</u> (N)
8. <u>loudly</u> (AV) <u>children</u> (N)
9. <u>loud</u> (A) <u>children</u> (N)

Lesson 35

Part C

1. <u>Henry</u> (N)
2. <u>often</u> (AV)
3. <u>friendly</u> (A)
4. <u>nervous</u> (A)
5. <u>rashes</u> (N)
6. <u>inside</u> (AV)
7. <u>clothes</u> (N)
8. <u>often</u> (AV)

Lesson 37

Part C

      A   N   V   AV
1. Five girls came here.

       A   N   V   A
2. Green butterflies are rare.

      A   N   V   A
3. Some boys are energetic.

      A   A   N   V   N
4. Those young women teach engineers.

      A   A   N   V AV
5. The delivery person is late.

      A   N   V   AV
6. Her dad speaks often.

      A   A   N   V   AV
7. Your oldest sister left yesterday.

      A   N   V   N
8. Their document presented information.

Lesson 38

Part B

      A   N   V   A
1. The horse was awkward.

      A   A   N   V   N
2. Those white birds are doves.

      N   V   AV
3. Billy swims well.

      A   A   N   V   AV
4. Our six candles burned quickly.

      A   N   V   N
5. That stove burns logs.

      N   V   N
6. Chimneys gather soot.

      A   N   V   A
7. Our assignment was difficult.

Lesson 39

Part F

      A   N   V   AV
1. My brother runs fast.

      A   N   V   A
2. His sister is pretty.

      A   N   V   N
3. Those boxes hold cups.

      A   A   N   V   AV
4. Seven curious ducks looked around.

      A   N   V   AV
5. The neighbors argued loudly.

Lesson 45

Part A

1. The traffic moved slowly.

3. He sat quietly.

5. They spoke softly.

6. She worked quickly.

10. She wrote neatly.

Lesson 45

Part E

1. According to the *Farmer's Almanac,* a lunar month is 29.531 days.

2. According to the *Hambone Atlas,* Bolivia is in South America.
   Or:
   According to the *Hambone Atlas,* Bolivia is on the South American continent.

3. According to the Internal Revenue Service, William Gleason earned $36,400 in 1990.

Lesson 47

Part C

1. flew high $\overset{\text{V \ AV}}{\text{flew high}}$
2. worked hard
3. is hard
4. held fast
5. is high

6. was close
7. is fast
8. sat together
9. huddled close

Lesson 48

Part B

3. We will build the house in March or in April.

   We will build the house in March or build the house in April.

   We will build the house in March, or we will build the house in April.

4. Water leaks from the ceiling and from the window.

   Water leaks from the ceiling and leaks from the window.

   Water leaks from the ceiling, and water leaks from the window.

Lesson 49

Part C

3. That dog sleeps, and it barks.

   Or:

   That dog sleeps, and that dog barks.

4. My uncle will visit on Monday, or he will visit on Tuesday.

   Or:

   My uncle will visit on Monday, or my uncle will visit on Tuesday.

Lesson 49

Part D

3. inconsistent

4. contradictory

Lesson 53

Part A

4. The noises of the train were irritating.

5. The odor of the smokestacks was terrible.

Lesson 53

Part D

2. The dog barked loudly.

5. Her coat protected thoroughly.

7. She spoke smoothly.

9. She ran smoothly.

Lesson 54

Part B

1. She spoke sweetly.

4. Our car runs quietly.

8. The announcer spoke loudly.

Lesson 54

Part C

1. The decisions of the group are surprising.

2. A disease of dogs is developing.

3. The efforts of Bob are weak.

4. The concentration of the girls is amazing.

5. The math performance of our students is good.

Lesson 55

Part A

1. The tones of Tom were sad.

2. The spokes of the wheel were rusty.

3. The performance of the bands was lively.

Lesson 56

Part A

1. The ruler of the islands was unfriendly.

2. The bosses of the crew were tough.

3. The mother of the children was hurrying home.

Lesson 64

Part E

[1] The Dunn Company decided to purchase a new copy machine. [2] **A committee made the decision.** [3] The committee recommended the Stinmore copy machine. [4] **Miss Thompson rejected this recommendation.** [5] **Miss Thompson preferred the Reemto copier.** [6] The committee recommended firing Miss Thompson. [7] Miss Thompson recommended firing the committee. [8] **The president of the Dunn Company ordered a meeting.** [9] The president ordered the committee to work with Miss Thompson. [10] The president told everybody to agree on one copy machine. [11] The committee met with Miss Thompson five times. [12] **The committee announced the name of the chosen machine.** [13] The Dunn Company purchased a Bleepo copier.

Lesson 65

Part C

[1] Mrs. Lee told her students to decide on a class project. [2] **The class considered seven projects.** [3] The class voted on those projects three times. [4] **The first vote ruled out two projects.** [5] The second vote ruled out one more project. [6] The class announced its choice by making a sign. [7] The sign said, "Keep our rivers clean." [8] The class was going to clean up a section of the Muddy River. [9] **Parents donated bags and tools.** [10] **Three trucks transported the students to the river.** [11] The students spent all day Saturday and Sunday picking up garbage. [12] **A reporter photographed them.** [13] An article about the clean-up appeared in the Wednesday newspaper. [14] **That article pleased the class.**

Lesson 67

Part B

The school council decided to clean up another part of the Muddy River. Mr. Parson's idea was to take rafts down the river. Another idea was to wade in the river and drag chains. The chains would collect junk. The council did not accept this plan. Some objections of the council were strong. Heidi's idea was to wear bright colors and life jackets, but we did not have enough life jackets. James thought that everybody should wear hats and heavy gloves.

Parts of Outline Diagrams

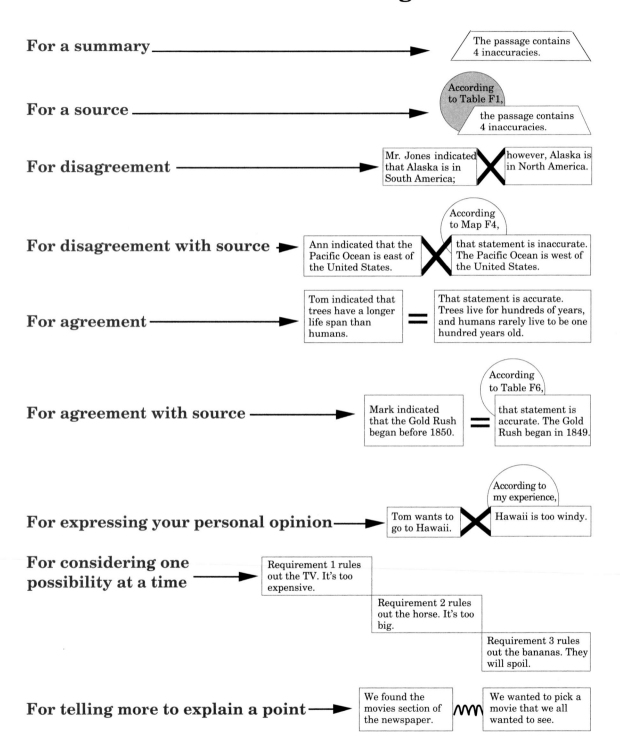

For a summary ⟶ The passage contains 4 inaccuracies.

For a source ⟶ According to Table F1, the passage contains 4 inaccuracies.

For disagreement ⟶ Mr. Jones indicated that Alaska is in South America; ✕ however, Alaska is in North America.

For disagreement with source ▶ Ann indicated that the Pacific Ocean is east of the United States. ✕ According to Map F4, that statement is inaccurate. The Pacific Ocean is west of the United States.

For agreement ⟶ Tom indicated that trees have a longer life span than humans. = That statement is accurate. Trees live for hundreds of years, and humans rarely live to be one hundred years old.

For agreement with source ⟶ Mark indicated that the Gold Rush began before 1850. = According to Table F6, that statement is accurate. The Gold Rush began in 1849.

For expressing your personal opinion ⟶ Tom wants to go to Hawaii. ✕ According to my experience, Hawaii is too windy.

For considering one possibility at a time ⟶ Requirement 1 rules out the TV. It's too expensive. Requirement 2 rules out the horse. It's too big. Requirement 3 rules out the bananas. They will spoil.

For telling more to explain a point ⟶ We found the movies section of the newspaper. ∿ We wanted to pick a movie that we all wanted to see.

Arguments

Correct Conclusion (Lesson 1)

| Argument __ concludes that _____ _____ ; | however, that conclusion does not follow from the evidence. |
| | The correct conclusion is that _____ . |

Other Possibilities (Lesson 2)

| _____ concluded that _____ _____ . | Another possibility is that _____ _____ . |

Conclusions More General Than the Evidence (Lesson 6)

| _____ concluded that _____ _____ . | however, the conclusion is more general than the evidence. Evidence about [specific category] cannot lead to a proper conclusion about [general category]. |

Part–Whole Fallacies (Lesson 26)

| Argument __ uses evidence about _____ to draw a conclusion about _____ . | However, evidence about (part/whole) does not lead to a proper conclusion about (another part/whole) . |

False Cause (Lesson 62)

_____ assumes that _____ cause _____ .

| The evidence is that _____ . | However, this evidence is inadequate. |

Adequate evidence would show that _____ _____ .

Misleading Claim (Lesson 68)

Paragraph 1

| _____ indicates that _____ ; | however, that claim is misleading. |
| If the claim was honest, _____ would _____ _____ . | However, _____ show that _____ _____ . |

Paragraph 2

| A fair way to compare _____ is to refer to _____ . | → | This method shows the following: _____ ; _____ _____ . |

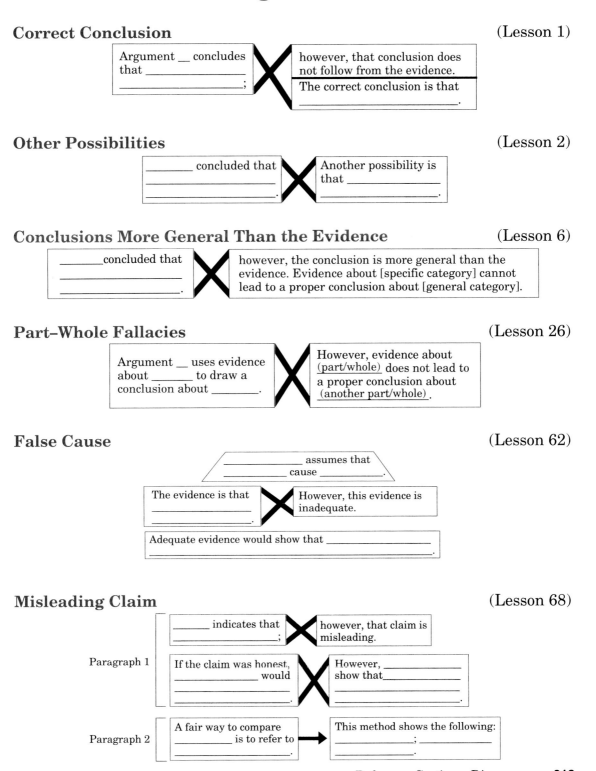

More Than One Requirement

(Lesson 3

_____ meets all of _____ requirements.

Requirement 1 rules out _____.
[Tell why.]

Requirement 2 rules out _____.
[Tell why.]

Requirement 3 rules out _____.
[Tell why.]

The remaining choice is _____.

Rule Testing

(Lesson 9

To test the rule, you could examine _____ _____.

If _____ _____, the evidence would discredit the rule.

If _____ _____, the evidence would not discredit the rule.

Compare and Contrast

(Lesson 16

According to _____,

_____ differs from _____ in ___ways.

1

2

3

1

2

3

1

2

3

Diagrams

Contradictions

(Lesson 46)

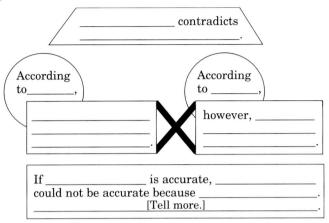